As a tree must have healthy roots to
in Christ. We are to be like 'trees firm
of God's Word. Rooted in Truth serv
compelling resource to help students deepen their biblical
thinking during a vital season of their lives.

GARRETT KELL
Pastor, Del Ray Baptist Church, Alexandria, Virginia

This book offers practical counsel firmly rooted in biblical fidelity and infused with personal care—both encouragement and caution—drawn from the authors' years of experience guiding college students through a crucial season of growth and spiritual maturity. A rich blend of wisdom and practice, it's a great read for any Christian stepping into this pivotal stage of life.

TREVIN WAX
Vice President, Resources and Marketing
North American Mission Board

You don't realize how risky parenting is until you send your kids to college. They step out into an atmosphere of strange winds—challenges they didn't know they'd face, and you've halfway forgotten. Thankfully, Rogers and Wood have lived out there with college students, learning how to guide them to old truth for new challenges. Exceptional.

JEREMY PIERRE
Professor of Biblical Counseling & Practical Theology
Southern Baptist Theological Seminary, Louisville, Kentucky

The college years are among the most formative years of our lives, with life decisions that set a trajectory for the future. They are also years where a worldview is contemplated and ultimately formed. To this end, Rooted in Truth is a principled and practical book that lays a solid foundation for college students in the formation of a biblical worldview. The book answers the most pressing questions that students have, including how to know God, how to choose a vocation, and what to look for in a future spouse. I'm excited to get this book into the hands of our high school and college students as they navigate such a pivotal season of life.

COREY ABNEY
Lead Pastor, Bell Shoals Church, Tampa, Florida

College years are the most pivotal season of your life. The decisions you make today will literally shape the rest of your life. Times and cultures continue to change, but the fundamental questions remain the same. This book offers practical, biblical answers to these enduring questions. An opportunity to hear God's unchanging truths amidst our ever-changing culture. Put down your digital devices and immerse yourself in its pages; it's goldmine wisdom to help navigate your most pressing concerns.

TROY NESBITT
President, The Salt Network

Jon and Trent have years of experience leading and ministering to college students. What they have put together in this book is a resource that answers life's most important questions to help the next generation build a solid foundation in Christ and His Word. As they prepare for the rest of their lives, reading and applying the wisdom found here will help young people move into adulthood confident in their faith and the Lord's leading in their lives.

KEVIN EZELL
President, North American Mission Board

Living and pastoring in a place like Salt Lake City, you get used to seeing people wrestle with truth claims and long for something solid to stand on. Rooted in Truth is the kind of book that meets students right there—with clarity, conviction, and compassion. Rogers and Wood write with a steady hand, offering biblical answers without assuming too much or talking down. Their chapters reflect years of thoughtful ministry to students in that vulnerable stretch of life just after leaving home. If you're a parent preparing your son or daughter for the challenges of adulthood, this is a wise and timely tool. It provides answers and a framework for thinking Christianly about work, friendship, sexuality, truth, and calling. The tone is pastoral, and the content is anchored deeply in Scripture, a valuable combination. I plan to commend it to students in our church and the parents raising them.

WILL GALKIN
Pastor of Outreach and Strategic Multiplication
Gospel Grace Church, Salt Lake City, Utah

Drawing on their years of experience in the university classroom and on campus, Dr. Rogers and Dr. Wood have delivered a Gospel-saturated, practically helpful resource to guide college students toward biblical discernment and wisdom. From the thoughtful selection of topics to the focused application of Scripture, Rogers and Wood lead the reader to think biblically and critically about the key worldview and life decisions that students face in these formative years.

BRIAN WHITE
Lead Pastor, Harvest Church, Carmel, Indiana

Answers to Life's Questions
for College Students

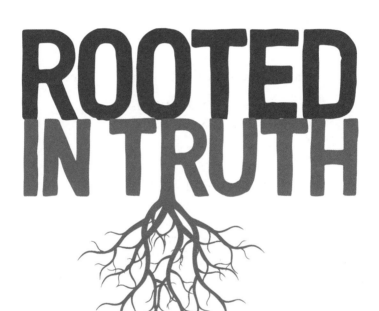
ROOTED IN TRUTH

Trent A. Rogers
& Jonathan A. Wood

CHRISTIAN FOCUS

Unless otherwise noted, Scripture quotations are from the ESV® Bible (The Holy Bible, English Standard Version®), copyright © 2001 by Crossway, a publishing ministry of Good News Publishers. Used by permission. All rights reserved.

Copyright © Trent A. Rogers / Jonathan A. Wood 2025

paperback ISBN 978-1-5271-1269-8
ebook ISBN 978-1-5271-1329-9

10 9 8 7 6 5 4 3 2 1

Published in 2025
by
Christian Focus Publications Ltd,
Geanies House, Fearn, Ross-shire,
IV20 1TW, Great Britain.

www.christianfocus.com

Cover design by
Pete Barnsley (CreativeHoot)

Printed and bound by
Bell & Bain, Glasgow

All rights reserved. No part of this publication may be reproduced, stored in a retrieval system, or transmitted, in any form, by any means, electronic, mechanical, photocopying, recording or otherwise without the prior permission of the publisher or a licence permitting restricted copying. In the U.K. such licences are issued by the Copyright Licensing Agency, 4 Battlebridge Lane, London, SE1 2HX. www.cla.co.uk

Contents

Introduction..ix

Part 1: Christian Living

   1. Gospel..1

   2. Bible 9

   3. Prayer..19

   4. Church..27

   5. Character..35

Part 2: Christian Vocation

   6. Life Purpose 47

   7. Work..57

   8. Wise Habits of Work..65

   9. Choosing a Major...73

   10. Great Commission Living 83

Part 3: Christian Apologetics

   11. Truth 93

   12. Authority..101

   13. Bible 111

   14. Humanity 121

   15. Exclusivity...131

Part 4: Christian Relationships and Dating

   16. Friendship 141

   17. Dating 151

   18. Marriage..159

   19. Discernment 1 167

   20. Discernment 2 175

Conclusion 185

Introduction

Farmland dominates our American Midwestern landscape. The flat fields stretch on for miles in parallel rows of beans and corn. In the growing season, the breeze can make the acres of corn appear as a sea of gentle green waves. And in the harvest season, the golden fields gleam in the sun. In some areas, these rolling plains of crops span out seemingly endlessly. Occasionally, in the middle of hundreds of acres of crops stands a giant, magnificent oak tree. Its outline provides such a contrast to everything around it. Protruding from the flat field is the trunk of a majestic tree that could have been growing for more than a century. Over the course of claiming and tilling the ground, all the lesser trees have been removed, but the oak stands firm. Each year, the crops come and go, but the oak stands firm. The prairie winds blow violently, but the oak stands firm. Some praise the majestic height of the redwood or the sequoia's girth, but the oak's strength is unparalleled. It stands alone in the fiercest of storms because its roots run deep. In the chaos of life, it is unmoved.

The mighty oak interrupting the landscape of impermanent growth provides a picture of stability that corresponds to a person rooted in the truth of God's Word. The Bible uses the image of a tree to present a life shaped by faith in God and serious study of His Word. "He is like a tree planted by streams of water that yields its fruit in its season, and its leaf does not wither. In all that he does, he prospers" (Ps. 1:3). Like the oak that weathers all the storms, the person who has deep-seated faith and whose roots are nourished in God's Word withstands the challenges and chaos of life. This person has the stability of the unmoving tree. He makes the right choices and "walks not in the counsel of the wicked" (1:1) but pursues the path of righteousness.

What leads to this stability and the ability to make wise decisions? The psalmist gives two grounding realities: delighting in God's Word and deep-seated faith in God's Deliverer. The psalmist introduces the Book of Psalms by telling us to dwell on God's Word (Ps. 1) and trust in God's Deliverer (Ps. 2). From the rest of the Bible, we recognize that the Deliverer, described as the King and God's Son in Psalm 2, is Jesus Christ (Acts 4:25-26; 13:33; Heb. 1:5; 5:5). The command to "kiss the Son" is a command to embrace His kingly rule, to submit to Him. So, the first and most important decision is to trust in Christ for salvation. When the apostles reflect on Psalm 2, they declare "that through this man forgiveness of sins is proclaimed to you" (Acts 13:38). Flowing from true faith is a desire for God's Word. The person who trusts in God's Son has new desires, and "his delight is in the law of the Lord, and on his law he meditates day and night" (1:2). What keeps this person stable, grounded, and persevering are his unflagging faith in the Son of God and unwavering commitment to God's Word.

Often, college years can be times of instability and uncertainty about one's faith. However, they can also be a time of significant spiritual growth and deepening faith. For both of us, college years dramatically affected our faith and set us on a trajectory of faith and ministry for the rest of our lives. Jon came to faith in the eighth grade from a non-Christian background and was never really rooted in discipleship through high school. Once at college, a church and college ministry imparting truth through biblical teaching and life-on-life discipleship transformed his trajectory. Trent's parents came to faith during college, changing the direction of the home where he grew up. Neither of us attended a Christian undergraduate school, but we have spent most of our professional lives ministering to college students at a Christian university.

Introduction

In our experience with various college ministries (at Christian and secular schools), we have seen that students from similar backgrounds can be radically different at the end of four years. What accounts for this difference? Why are the college years a catalyst for Christian growth for some and a cause of struggle for others? The burden of our hearts is to help you to grow in your faith during your college years. We pray that when you graduate, you will be characterized by steadfast faith. Our prayer is that you will not be moved by every new thought, cultural movement, or peer pressure that you meet. We pray that you will be planted in truth so that you are steadfast and stable.

We have written this book to help plant students in the Christian Scriptures and faith in the Christian Deliverer. We want to see them choose the path of righteousness. We encourage students to believe in God and dwell on His Word. College presents students with new decisions and the latest ideas, and students have questions. This book is our attempt to root students in the Scriptures and explain the paths of righteousness and wickedness. It is a combination of explanation of Scripture and wisdom drawn from decades of ministry to college students.

Each chapter aims to be an accessible introduction to a topic that merits a deeper discussion. We expect that many readers will want fuller treatment of many of these topics, and those larger volumes are available. The book has four categories, each with five chapters: Christian Living, Christian Vocation, Christian Apologetics, and Christian Relationships and Dating. Each chapter concludes with reflection questions that could be useful for the reader personally or in a small group setting.

We wrote this book prayerfully to help ground you in biblical truth and wisdom. Our prayer for you is that you will be ROOTED IN TRUTH.

Part 1

Christian Living

1

Gospel

How do I become a Christian?

Have you ever seen someone's life change in radical ways? I am not talking about some superficial or contrived change, but a change that transforms a person's core so that his hopes and desires are different. When I (Trent) was in high school, I served in the greeting ministry at my church. A visitor came to church one day. He was not hard to spot as a visitor because he did not know where to go, seemed nervous, used more colorful language, and told stories about life choices that were not following the Lord. He was struggling to make a connection until he spotted Danny. Danny was a deacon in the church who radiated godliness and servant-heartedness. When he saw Danny, his face lit up, and his demeanor changed—he had made a connection and felt like he could stay. His next statement shocked me, "If Danny can be a Christian, then anybody can." To me, Danny was the picture of godliness and following the Lord. But he and Danny had been close friends before Danny became a Christian. He did not know about the radical life change in Danny's life. In that church lobby, there stood two men who could not be more different in their lifestyles and their deepest hopes. But twenty years earlier, their lives were indistinguishable. Danny had come to faith in Jesus, and his life had been transformed. This is what is often called conversion.

The term "conversion" carries different connotations across cultures. In the West, "conversion" rings of arrogant and abusive colonialism. In the Middle East, "conversion" can be punishable with severe consequences, even death. However, "conversion" simply means moving from one position or state to another. In some contexts (e.g., converting currency or biochemical bodily processes), conversion is not freighted with such weight and heightened emotion. However, in the context of a person's most closely held beliefs and identity, it is right for "conversion" to be recognized as a term of utmost significance. In the religious context, conversion is the fundamental changing of allegiance—the complete reorientation of one's life.

"Conversion," or becoming a Christian, is not a new issue. For nearly two millennia, Christians have told others of the truth about Jesus Christ and how he has changed their lives. It can be asked, "How do I become a Christian?" But that question really does not get to the motivation for change. Before someone asks "How?" he is likely to ask "Why?" So often the most critical response is to answer the question of "Why should I become a Christian." As the message about Jesus Christ comes to new ears, this has often been the question because the message about Jesus calls for a response. One of the first people to understand the reality about Jesus, exclaimed, "'What must I do to be saved?'" (Acts 16:30). If, as this man realized, salvation is at stake, then the answer to this question is of the utmost importance. The response is just as straightforward as the question: "Believe in the Lord Jesus, and you will be saved" (Acts 16:31). Although the response is simple, the response and the question assume answers to several other questions. From what do I need to be saved? Who is Jesus? How has He provided salvation? What does it mean to believe?

What is the gospel?

To answer these questions, we need to think about the Bible as a whole, not merely one dialogue recorded in the Book of Acts. The central message of Christianity is the gospel. "Gospel" means good news. And in the Christian sense of "gospel," it is the good news about Jesus. We might say it simply: the gospel is the good news that God saves sinners through Jesus Christ. The gospel primarily focuses on the death and resurrection of Jesus and declares that the kingdom of God has come. This is not a new message. It is the message that Jesus came to proclaim. Mark describes the ministry of Jesus in this way: Jesus came into Galilee, proclaiming the gospel of God, and saying, "The time is fulfilled, and the kingdom of God is at hand; repent and believe in the gospel" (Mark 1:14-15). The gospel is the message about the saving activity of God explained in four acts: God's creation, humanity's rebellion, God's provision, and humanity's response. In short, we might describe the significant movements in this drama as God-Human-God-Human.

GOD

God designed the world so that He might have a relationship with humanity. From the first human beings down to every person alive today, God loves and blesses human beings. With the first humans, the Bible describes this relationship as them existing with God in an idyllic garden called Eden. God showed them who He was and how to relate to Him. And God continues to reveal something about Himself to all people through what is seen in nature: "For what can be known about God is plain to them, because God has shown it to them. For his invisible attributes, namely, his eternal power and divine nature, have been clearly perceived, ever since the creation of the world, in the things that have been made" (Rom. 1:19-20). People should respond to this revelation of God by worshipping Him as God and seeking to know Him. They should embrace a relationship with God and worship Him.

HUMAN

Tragically, the beauty and glory of this relationship was marred by humanity's rebellion against God. Instead of reveling in the joy of a relationship with God, human beings reject that relationship and seek their own way. Beginning with the first humans, and including every human being after them, people have sinned against God and rejected any relationship with Him. The tragic human story is one of seeking purpose, fulfillment, and meaning apart from God, and coming up empty. God's response to Adam and Eve's rebellion involves both just judgment and astounding grace. Because God is holy and without sin, He is angry with them about their sin. He removes them from His presence and expresses His just wrath toward them.

One consequence of man's sin is death, both physically and spiritually, in becoming distanced from God. Romans 3:22–23 explains that all people sin and thus are incapable of life with God: "For there is no distinction: for all have sinned and fall short of the glory of God…" Moreover, "…the wages of sin is death…" (Rom. 6:23). That is, life is the reward of a relationship with God and humans have earned death for themselves by severing their relationship with God. People are as bad off as they could be, wallowing in sin, under the wrath of God, and incapable of helping themselves. Humanity, along with all creation, is marred by this fall into sin. When death and degradation enter the world, their effects spread beyond humanity.

GOD

The story could end with all people condemned justifiably for their sins. But God's story does not end in death: "For the wages of sin is death, but the free gift of God is eternal life in Christ Jesus our Lord" (Rom. 3:23). God the Father sent God the Son in the power of God the Spirit to redeem humanity and restore all creation—the Triune God sets out to rescue. The Son of God came to live as a human and bear the penalty that their sin deserves (Phil. 2:5–11). He died a gruesome death on the cross in their place. The Bible describes this as the great exchange: our guilt for Jesus' pardon, our sin for Jesus' righteousness: "For our sake he made him to be sin who knew

Gospel

no sin, so that in him we might become the righteousness of God" (2 Cor. 5:21).

God's Son, Jesus, is the Author of life, and death is powerless over Him. He rose from the dead and lives victoriously. The gospel promises that we can share in and enjoy Jesus' resurrection victory. Humanity can have life with God because God in Christ has made it possible: "God shows his love for us in that while we were still sinners, Christ died for us. Since, therefore, we have now been justified by his blood, much more shall we be saved by him from the wrath of God" (Rom. 5:8-9). It is crucial to understand that the work of salvation is not something that any mere human could accomplish. Jesus Christ as fully human (and thus able to stand in our place and die) and fully God (and thus able to bear God's wrath completely and overcome death victoriously) accomplished the work of salvation. That is the good news of the gospel—Jesus Christ has done what we could not. The gospel is about the work of God in Christ, especially His death and resurrection, to provide salvation for all people who trust in him.

HUMAN

If Jesus accomplished this salvation, does that mean everyone experiences salvation and new life in Jesus Christ? The Bible tells us that while the gospel is available to every person, not every person experiences salvation. The gospel demands a response. Recall what Paul said to the Philippian jailor, "'Believe in the Lord Jesus, and you will be saved'" (Acts 16:31). The gospel demands that every person respond in repentance and faith. Repentance is turning from sin and turning to God. It involves the recognition that the promises of sin are false and hollow and the recognition that God is true and all-satisfying. Faith is deciding to depend on Jesus for salvation. It involves the recognition that nothing of this world can provide meaning to life and provide everlasting life. Elsewhere Paul describes the response like this: "If you confess with your mouth that Jesus is Lord and believe in your heart that God raised him from the dead, you will be saved" (Rom. 10:9). And the promise God gives us is that "For 'everyone who calls on the name of the Lord will be saved'" (Rom. 10:13). Although the call to believe in Jesus involves understanding and recognizing certain assertions about Jesus (truly God, truly human, substitutionary death, resurrection), the call to believe involves the complete trust of one's whole heart in Jesus Christ.

How does the gospel change one's life?

One of the promises of the gospel is that those who trust in Jesus Christ have eternal life: "whoever believes in him may have eternal life" (John 3:15). Eternal life is not merely a quantity (ongoing forever) of life, but a quality of life. Even though the fullness of eternal life with God awaits a future realization, the Christian begins to live that new life now. In Ephesians 1, Paul reminds Christians of their identity "in Christ." Christians have a deep and inseparable relationship with Christ by faith, so a *Christ*ian's identity is tied up with *Christ*. Christians are blessed by God (1:3, 5), chosen by God (1:4), adopted into God's family (1:5), forgiven by the work of Christ (1:7), indwelt by the Holy Spirit (1:13), and promised an eternal inheritance (1:11, 14). The reality of this transformation is so comprehensive that Paul can say that Christians are completely new: "if anyone is in Christ, he is a new creation. The old has passed away; behold, the new has come" (2 Cor. 5:17).

This union with Christ is an intimate identification with Christ in His life, death, burial and resurection. It is a trust in these realities that results in new life and a new way of living. Paul describes this transformation: "We were buried therefore with him by baptism into death, so that, just as Christ was raised from the dead by the glory of the Father, we too might walk in newness of life" (Rom. 6:4). We must understand that we live a transformed life in Christ because we have already been transformed by the power of the Spirit (Rom. 8:11). Another way to say this is that someone who has been freed is motivated out of gratitude to live in freedom. Returning to Paul's argument in Ephesians, because Jesus Christ has saved Christians, they "walk in a manner worthy of the calling to which you have been called, with all humility and gentleness, with patience, bearing with one another in love, eager to maintain the unity of the Spirit in the bond of peace" (Eph. 4:1–3).

So, a Christian is a new creation through the work of Jesus Christ, and that Christian now lives differently. But since a Christian is not saved by his own good deeds, what motivates him to live in a new way? In Ephesians, Paul repeatedly describes salvation and the Christian life as oriented "to the praise of his glory" (1:6, 12, 14). What God has done in salvation brings God glory and provides the motivation for Christian living. Paul states this motivation succinctly: "whatever you do, do all to the glory of God" (1 Cor. 10:31).

Conclusion

The gospel message is the singular message that makes sense of the world, gives real meaning to our lives, and holds the promise of eternal life. Some messages are not crucial to get exactly right. If my wife asks me to buy a turkey and I mistakenly get a ham, that might be irresponsible, but we'll still have dinner. But some messages are so significant that they result in either life or death. The gospel is the message of the greatest significance with the greatest promise. Believe in Jesus today!

Reflection Questions:

1. Have you responded to this gospel message of salvation by repenting of sin and believing in Jesus Christ?
2. When you think about the promises of the gospel (e.g., forgiveness, restoration to right relationship with God, freedom from sin, adoption into God's family, etc.), which ones stand out to you as the sweetest? Why?

3. Are there aspects of the gospel you do not understand? Is there a pastor or a trusted Christian you can talk with about what you do not understand?
4. How does a response of faith in Jesus and repentance from sin influence everyday aspects of your life?

2

Bible

How do I know God?

We do not learn everything in the same way. Some things we learn by experience, others by observation, and others by talking to people. Some knowledge exceeds our physical ability to see. For example, a person needs specific instruments to see the smallest particles. Similarly, a person needs specific instruments to see the largest planetary bodies at extreme distances. For matters of knowledge that we obtain through observation, highly specialized instruments help us. But what about knowledge that cannot be obtained merely through observation? How we know something is moral or beautiful is not simply through physical perception.

Even while we acknowledge that we come to know some things in different ways, knowledge of God might belong to its own category. God is not like anything else in the world, so it should not surprise us that we do not come to know God in the same ways that we know everything else. Sometimes, people use the term "transcendent" to describe God. The word "transcendent" describes how God is beyond our ability to fully understand or comprehend. God is so amazing and so magnificent that He alone is sufficient to reveal Himself. Stated another way, we must rely on God to make Himself known. We cannot reason our way to God. Nor can we observe our way to God. He must choose to interact with us.

Even while knowing God is different than other forms of knowledge and we are utterly dependent on God to make Himself known, we must also realize that the knowledge of God is the most precious reality in the world. God declares: "Thus says the Lord: 'Let not the wise man boast in his wisdom, let not the mighty man boast in his might, let not the rich man boast in his riches, but let him who boasts boast in this, that he understands and knows me, that I am the Lord who practices steadfast love, justice, and righteousness in the earth. For in these things I delight, declares the Lord" (Jer. 9:23–24). One of the earliest Christians, Paul, claimed something similar when he said his greatest desire was "that I may know him [Jesus Christ] and the power of his resurrection..." (Phil. 3:10). Since knowledge about God is so precious, we must pursue that knowledge rightly and diligently.

How does God make Himself known?

If we are honest, there is something within us that already knows the existence of God. There is a yearning in us beyond what this world can produce. C. S. Lewis noted this reality about human desires: "If we find ourselves with a desire that nothing in this world can satisfy, the most probable explanation is that we were made for another world."[1] Even by observing the world and our own consciences, we understand that God exists: "what can be known about God is plain to them [i.e. all humanity], because God has shown it to them" (Rom. 1:19). Paul claims that God has revealed something about His existence in the hearts of people, and also He has shown them that He exists by the wonder of the natural world: "For his invisible attributes, namely, his eternal power and divine nature, have been clearly perceived, ever since the creation of the world, in the things that have been made. So they are without excuse" (Rom. 1:20). From what we observe in nature and humanity, we can see that God exists and so understand

---

1. C. S. Lewis, *Mere Christianity* (New York: HarperOne, 2001), 136.

Bible

some things about Him. This awareness comes from what is called general (or natural) revelation.

But there are limits to what the natural world can tell us about God. For example, from observing the natural world, we know that God exists, but not that God exists as Father, Son, and Spirit. Similarly, while general revelation shows us that God acts in the world, we do not know that the Father sent the Son as savior of the world. For us to know some realities about God, we need Him to reveal Himself beyond what He does through what is observable to all people in general revelation. We need God's special revelation of Himself. God has revealed Himself in special ways through His acts in history, and preeminently, He has revealed Himself through His Son: "Long ago, at many times and in many ways, God spoke to our fathers by the prophets, but in these last days he has spoken to us by his Son, whom he appointed the heir of all things, through whom also he created the world" (Heb. 1:1–2; see also John 1:18; 14:8–10). In the subsequent verses, the Book of Hebrews identifies the Son of God as Jesus Christ. The follow-up question is, then, how do we come to know about the Son, Jesus Christ? We are not currently experiencing the earthly ministry of Jesus. God has chosen for us to come to know about His Son through the written words of the Bible. These statements in Hebrews 1 and John 1 assert that God reveals Himself through His Son, and then both books go on to describe the Son. The implication is that the Bible accurately communicates the Son to us in written words.

What is the Bible?

So God reveals Himself through His Son and we have access to this revelation about His Son through the written words of the Bible (sometimes called "Scripture"). What, then, can we say that the Bible is? An important description of the Bible is found in 2 Timothy 3:16–17: "All Scripture is breathed out by God and profitable for teaching, for reproof, for correction, and for training in righteousness, that the man of God may be complete, equipped for every good work." Two observations are crucial for us to understand the Bible rightly. When Paul says "all Scripture," he has in mind a group of writings. Certainly, he means the Scriptures of the Old Testament. But even while the New Testament was still being written early on, other New Testament writings became recognized as Scripture as well (see 2 Pet. 3:14–16). So, when we talk about Scripture, we mean the sixty-six books of the Old and New Testaments.

Remarkably, the words of these books are "breathed out by God." That is, they are the very words of God. When humans speak, we breathe out air. When God spoke, He breathed out the Scriptures (often called the inspiration of Scripture). Inspiration also entails that the words have the character of the One who said them. For example, since God is truthful and wise, His words in the Bible are truthful and wise. God also intends to accomplish something through His words in Scripture. Scripture functions among believers to produce "complete" or mature Christians who perform good works (Col. 1:28–29).

The qualities we have already affirmed about Scripture (revelatory, inspired, truthful), have other implications of what we must affirm about Scripture. First, Scripture is inerrant (see Pss. 12:6; 18:30; Prov. 30:5; Matt. 5:18; 24:35; John 10:35; 17:17; Heb. 6:18). Inerrancy is grounded in God's truthfulness and capability. He speaks truth, and He can communicate that truth to us. Gregg Allison provides the following definition: "Truthfulness (inerrancy) is an attribute of Scripture by which whatever it affirms corresponds to reality, and it never affirms anything that is contrary to fact."[2] There might be other documents in the world that are without error, but Scripture cannot err because it is the very words of God himself, who cannot err (what some call infallibility).

There are a few more qualities of Scripture that Christians affirm, and they can be remembered with the acronym SCAN:

---

2. Gregg R. Allison, *50 Core Truths of the Christian Faith: A Guide to Understanding and Teaching Theology* (Grand Rapids: Baker, 2018), 16.

Bible

sufficiency, clarity, authority, and necessity.[3] While the Bible does not speak about every subject or contain all truth, the Bible contains everything we need to know and love God (sufficiency). While some things in the Bible require deeper study, the Bible in general is understandable to Christians because the Spirit indwells them, and they can work hard to interpret it faithfully (clarity). While there are many truth claims made around us, the Bible stands over all our thoughts and actions (authority). Even though God reveals some things about Himself in general revelation, the Bible is essential for us to love and obey God (necessity).

How should I read the Bible?

As we have described the nature of the Bible, the implication is that a Christian ought to be eager to engage the Bible and have a heart disposition to desire God's Word. From a practical standpoint, that also means that we need a plan. To accomplish anything of significance in our lives, we need structure and a plan. Imagine someone with a goal to be physically fit. That person must have a plan that he or she enacts faithfully to accomplish the goal of fitness. Similarly, the person who desires to know and obey God's Word—to be a Word-shaped person—needs to have a plan for how he or she will engage God's Word daily. There are many good Bible-reading plans, and some people like to rotate or change plans. The point is to be intentional about your pursuit of knowing and obeying God.

Just as important as the intentionality of engaging God's Word is the disposition of your heart that you bring to reading the Bible. Without the eyes of faith and humble dependence on the Spirit of God, one can misread the Bible and not experience its intended effect. For example, Jesus rebuked some religious leaders of His day because they searched the Scriptures but missed the point. The point of the Scriptures is

---

3. I first saw them presented as an acronym by Kevin DeYoung, *Taking God at His Word: Why the Bible is Knowable, Necessary, and Enough, and What that Means for You and Me* (Wheaton: Crossway, 2014), 44.

13

to *point* to Jesus. But, in their jealous and unbelieving hearts, they rejected Jesus (see John 5:39–40). It is vital that we read the Bible carefully and with the right interpretive approach. This is what some have called hermeneutics. While we cannot discuss a detailed approach to hermeneutics in this book, we do want to highlight a few dispositions of the heart with which a Christian should approach the Bible.

PRAYERFULLY

The kind of change that we want to see in our hearts in response to God's word is a change that can only come through God changing our hearts. What is supernatural about a Christian reading the Bible is that the indwelling Spirit guides and shapes the Christian. While there are many ways that the Bible is like other books, there are significant ways in which the Bible is unique. It is divine communication from God Himself, and God Himself through His Spirit enables the Christian to read and respond rightly to the Word. I often begin my Bible reading time with this short prayer: "Open my eyes, that I may behold wondrous things out of your law" (Ps. 119:18).

HUMBLY

Reading the Bible rightly requires that we never lose sight of who is speaking. In the Bible, God speaks, so the Bible carries the authority of God's speech. That recognition must shape our disposition to the Bible in that we understand ourselves to be in submission to the authority of God's Word because we are in submission to the authority of God. The book of James reminds us to "be doers of the word, and not hearers only, deceiving yourselves" (1:22). Someone who merely reads the Bible but does not have a humble heart posture to obey it shows that he has not rightly understood God, himself, or the Bible. In our house, we begin family devotions by asking that James 1:22 would be true of us. We want God to shape our lives through His word.

JOYFULLY

Too often, we lose sight of the privilege of reading God's Word. One of the challenges of the Christian life is that we all experience times when our hearts are not as excited about the things of God as we would want to be. If you experience these times, do not become discouraged. Humbly pray (see above) that God would shape your heart. Too often we forget that the Bible shows us the source of our joy, God Himself. Because we delight in knowing God, and the Bible is the way to know God, reading the Bible becomes a source of joy for the Christian.

Psalm 119 is the most extended section in the Bible about the Bible. And one of the most remarkable things in this chapter is the description of joy the believer has in the written words of God: "In the way of your testimonies I delight as much as in all riches. I will meditate on your precepts and fix my eyes on your ways. I will delight in your statutes; I will not forget your word" (vv. 14–16; see also vv. 20, 24, 35, 40, 43, 47, 48, 70, 92, 97, 103, 111, 119, 127, 129, 159, 162, 163, 174). The psalmist is a model for us of treasuring God's Word because we treasure God.

DAILY

The Book of Psalms begins by extolling the virtues of the Scripture-shaped life: "Blessed is the man who walks not in the counsel of the wicked, nor stands in the way of sinners, nor sits in the seat of scoffers; but His delight is in the law of the Lord, and on his law he meditates day and night" (Ps. 1:1–2). The way that Psalm 1 describes the Scripture-shaped life is reminiscent of God's instruction to His people in Deuteronomy 6:5–9: "You shall love the Lord your God with all your heart and with all your soul and with all your might. And these words that I command you today shall be on your heart. You shall teach them diligently to your children, and shall talk of them when you sit in your house, and when you walk by the way, and when you lie down, and when you rise.

You shall bind them as a sign on your hand, and they shall be as frontlets between your eyes. You shall write them on the doorposts of your house and on your gates." Delight in God directs us to daily engagement with His Word. This is not to say that if a Christian does not read the Bible on a given day, that the day is an utter failure. Again, we are instructing about the postures of the heart. And our disposition ought to be the daily desire to delight in God's Word.

CORPORATELY

Most of the writings in the New Testament were composed first for churches. This means that most commands addressed to "you" in the New Testament are addressed to "you all." English does not have a commonly used expression to communicate "you all" (unless you are from the American South, in which you would say "all y'all"). Recall that Paul says that all Scripture is inspired by God, and thus "profitable for teaching, for reproof, for correction, and for training in righteousness..." (2 Tim. 3:16). These are interpersonal activities in which someone uses the Scriptures to teach, reprove, correct, and train. The point is that by His Word, God has called a people to Himself, and He intends them to be a Word-shaped people.

MISSIONALLY

To read the Bible "corporately" means that we read the Bible with other Christians to grow in our Christian faith. To read the Bible "missionally" or "evangelistically" means that we read the Bible with non-Christians to see them believe in the Christian faith (see Acts 17:2–3). Many non-Christians are open to the idea of reading a book with someone else because "book clubs" are already a cultural practice. You might begin by asking a non-believer or a group of non-believers to read Mark or John with you. You could meet at a neutral place like a coffee shop or an inviting place like your apartment or dorm. As you read together, you can answer their questions about Jesus and pray that God awakens their hearts to believe in Jesus.

Conclusion

We became Christians when God "shone in our hearts to give the light of the knowledge of the glory of God in the face of Jesus Christ" (2 Cor. 4:6). This happens by the Spirit enabling our hearts to receive God's Word that contains the gospel of Jesus Christ. Apart from the testimony of God's Word and the work of the Spirit, we could never see "the light of the gospel of the glory of Christ, who is the image of God" (2 Cor. 4:4). That is, God has called us to faith in His Son through the Scriptures (i.e. special revelation), and He intends for us to live out that faith through a Scripture-shaped life.

Early in my Christian walk, I heard a quote about a Christian and the Bible: "A Bible that is falling apart usually belongs to someone who isn't."[4] The idea is that a person who constantly dwells on God's word is transformed by God. And this person becomes characterized by stability and wisdom. I can attest that I found that quote to be true in my own life and in the lives of others. Maturing Christians are disciplined in reading the Bible and have the heart posture of joyfully hearing from God.

Reflection Questions

1. Which of these dispositions of the heart would you most like to grow in with respect to your Bible reading: prayerfully, humbly, joyfully, daily, corporately, missionally?
2. How is the Bible both like and unlike other books?
3. With whom can you gather with on occasion to discuss your Bible reading for fellowship and encouragement?
4. What aspects of the Bible's nature (inspired, sufficient, clarity, authority, and necessity) freshly influences the way you think about knowing God?

---

4.   I later learned that this quote is attributed to Charles Spurgeon.

3

Prayer

How do I relate to God?

Historically, churches have held prayer meetings. This is a time when the church gathers, not to talk to one another, but to talk to God. Imagine being an atheist stumbling upon a prayer meeting at a church. It would seem strange to see a bunch of people talking to someone who cannot be seen. Now let's envision another scenario. Let's imagine that you're a Christian and you attend a church service in another town. There's a warm welcome from the members, vibrant teaching, and even some formal elements of the church, such as baptism and the Lord's Supper, but there was no prayer in this church. It would seem strange, even ridiculous. The reason that both scenarios are strange is because prayer only makes sense if you believe that God exists, hears the prayers of His people, wants to respond, and can respond. To the atheist who denies the reality of God, prayer is talking to someone who does not exist. To the Christian who affirms the personal God who desires a relationship with His people, prayer is a special privilege and natural outflow of that relationship.

What is prayer?
We have already seen that prayer is rooted in faith because it assumes the existence of God and His desire to interact with His people. When we say that prayer assumes the existence of God, we mean the existence of the Christian God, so that

19

Christian prayer is Trinitarian prayer—*to* the Father *through* the Son *in* the Spirit. In many of the longer prayers in the New Testament, we see this pattern. For example, Paul addresses his prayers to the Father with reference to the work of the Son: "I thank my God through Jesus Christ" (Rom. 1:8); "I give thanks to my God always for you because of the grace of God that was given to you in Christ Jesus" (1 Cor. 1:4); "Blessed be the God and Father of our Lord Jesus Christ, who has blessed us in Christ with every spiritual blessing in the heavenly places" (Eph. 1:3); "We always thank God, the Father of our Lord Jesus Christ, when we pray for you, since we heard of your faith in Christ Jesus..." (Col. 1:3–4). Paul's ability to address the Father as a son is grounded in the work of the one and only Son, Jesus Christ. And in the immediate context of these prayers, Paul typically references the work of the Holy Spirit, so that Christian prayer is "praying at all times in the Spirit" (Eph. 6:18; see also Jude 20).

One group of Christians defined prayer as "pouring out our hearts to God in praise, petition, confession of sin, and thanksgiving."[1] Biblical prayer is more diverse than merely asking God to act; it involves confession, blessing, adoration, thanksgiving, lament, etc. In this summary of how the Bible presents prayer, we see that while prayer is relational communication similar to how we might interact with other people, there are remarkable differences because God is unlike anyone else. God is holy and transcendent; He is so completely beyond us that we are unable to relate to Him unless He makes a way. The Bible describes our access to God the Father in prayer as being through the work of Jesus Christ and in the Spirit, "For through him [i.e. Jesus Christ] we both have access in one Spirit to the Father" (Eph. 2:18; see also Rom. 8:15–17). This is what Christians mean when they say their prayers "in Jesus' name." They are praying (1) in acknowledgment that their access to God is only through the work of Jesus and (2) in line with what Jesus would have us

---

1. New City Catechism Q. 38

Prayer

pray for. Jesus promises that "whatever you ask of the Father in my name, he will give it to you. Until now you have asked nothing in my name. Ask, and you will receive, that your joy may be full" (John 16:23–24). As we have seen, prayer is also in the Spirit, so that we are led in prayerful communication that is not merely one-way: "Likewise the Spirit helps us in our weakness. For we do not know what to pray for as we ought, but the Spirit himself intercedes for us with groanings too deep for words" (Rom. 8:26).

So prayer is a way that God has designed for His people to communicate with Him. The way that unholy and finite creatures can have access to the holy and infinite God is through the work of God's Son and Spirit. The Son of God, through His substitutionary work, makes it possible for us to address the Father as children. The Spirit of God, through His intercession, leads us in praying rightly.

Why should we pray?

While prayer is communication, it is unlike any other form of communication because it is communication with a person unlike any other. Sometimes, Christians wonder why they should pray if God already knows everything and desires to provide for their needs. In the Bible, God gives us some reasons that we ought to pray. The most straightforward reason that we should pray is because God commands it. "Rejoice always, pray without ceasing, give thanks in all circumstances; for this is the will of God in Christ Jesus for you. Do not quench the Spirit" (1 Thess. 5:16–19; see also John 16:24; Col. 4:2). This pattern of a prayer-filled life is what Jesus modeled. His pattern amid the busyness of ministry was to devote time to prayer: "But he would withdraw to desolate places to pray" (Luke 5:16). In prayer, we follow the example of the Son and relate to God as His children. And God delights in the prayers of His people (e.g., Prov. 15:8; Rev. 5:7–8).

Prayer not only brings us closer to God but also transforms us. It shapes our desires to align with God's will, brings us joy as we see Him answer, and deepens our trust in His timing and wisdom. God promises "that if we ask anything according to his will he hears us. And if we know that he hears us in whatever we ask, we know that we have the requests that we have asked of him" (1 John 5:14–15). This promise compels us to evaluate our prayers to discern if they are for the kinds of things that God desires to give. God shapes us by training us, through the ministry of the Spirit and the Scriptures, in what we ought to pray. Praying "according to his will" or in the name of Jesus leads to our joy because God responds to our prayers (John 16:24). How remarkable is it that God has ordered the world in such a way that He responds to the prayers of His people? While we do not fully understand how it works for God to plan and control everything and still listen and respond to prayer, we have confidence that God does (e.g., Matt. 7:7–11).

How should we pray?

Christians should have a heart posture to relate to God in prayer regularly. Scripture calls this praying "without ceasing": "Rejoice always, pray without ceasing, give thanks in all circumstances; for this is the will of God in Christ Jesus for you. Do not quench the Spirit" (1 Thess. 5:16–19). Praying without ceasing does not mean that we lock ourselves in our rooms and do nothing but pray. That would make it impossible to fulfill many of the other commands in Scripture, such as serving one another. Instead, praying without ceasing is an awareness and disposition of the heart to interact with God as always present. Praying without ceasing throughout one's day is also consistent with having dedicated prayer times. In fact, dedicated times of prayer often fuel the practice of ceaseless and ongoing prayer throughout the day. Again, Jesus is our model as He unceasingly interacted with the Father while also having specific times dedicated to uninterrupted prayer. Often, Christians ask how they can develop a more prayerful life. The answer is both the consistent prayer of a dedicated time and the ceaseless prayer of a dependent awareness. Start with a dedicated time, perhaps using a list or journal of requests, and see how God develops a heart of ceaseless prayer.

Christians should also pray with perseverance. Often, we become discouraged in our prayers. We pray for things that we are confident God wants to bring about, but then it seems like God does not respond, or at least not in the way we wanted or expected. One pastor gave this helpful counsel about dealing with disappointment and confusion in prayer: "God will either give us what we ask or give us what we would have asked if we knew everything he knows."[2] If we were like God—perfectly good, knowing all things, and capable of accomplishing anything—we would grant to Christians the very things that God gives us and in the exact timing that He does. The challenge is that we do not know everything that God knows, and our desires are not always perfectly good. So even when our prayers are not answered in the way that we wanted, we keep praying while asking God to align our hearts with his.

Jesus knew that prayer requires perseverance, so "he told them a parable to the effect that they ought always to pray and not lose heart" (Luke 18:1; see also Rom. 15:30). The hyperbolic story that Jesus tells involves a woman who keeps bringing her request to a wicked judge. Even though the judge is wicked and does not care for the woman, he nevertheless responds to her because of her persistence. How much more does our loving Father hear and is eager to respond to the prayers of His people! The conclusion to this story is a call for Christians to have persevering faith in their prayers.

Christians also need to listen to Jesus' teaching about the joy of prayer. In John 16, Jesus instructs Christians to pray with anticipation of His return. This anticipation in prayer requires perseverance, but it should be done in a joy-filled manner. Jesus told His disciples, "Until now you have asked nothing in my name. Ask, and you will receive, that your joy may be full" (John 16:24). How does prayer lead to Christians having full

---

2. Tim Keller, *Prayer: Experiencing Awe and Intimacy with God* (New York: Dutton, 2014), 228.

joy? One aspect of our joy in prayer comes simply in relating to God. We were created for a relationship with God, and expressing that intimate relationship is a joy-filled practice. Another aspect of our joy in praying is seeing God answer our requests. We ask; He responds, and our joy increases.

There are many ways to pursue a strong prayer life, but here are a few ideas to get you started.

CORPORATELY

Prayer is not merely the way that Christians relate personally to God. When you gather as the church, actively engage as another leads in prayer. Also, find ways to engage with other Christians in prayer in contexts such as small Bible study groups. Private prayer complements corporate prayer, and vice versa. It can be challenging to pray with others because our minds can be prone to wander. Even those who prayed with Jesus sometimes found it difficult to focus (Matt. 26:40–46). Try to engage your mind and heart in these times of prayer and remind yourself of the importance of prayer and praying with others.

WITH SCRIPTURE

Reading Scripture before praying reminds us of who God is and how we should relate to Him rightly. We also encourage the practice of praying the prayers recorded in Scripture. God has chosen for certain prayers (e.g., the psalms and the openings to many of the New Testament epistles, etc.) to be in the inspired text of Scripture. These prayers instruct us on how to pray, and we can pray these prayers back to God. Praying Scripture also helps us engage more senses to keep us alert and instructs us in the kinds of things for which we ought to pray. I make it a personal practice to pray Colossians 1:3–14 for members of my church.

THE LORD'S PRAYER

The best-known of the prayers in Scripture is the Lord's Prayer. When Jesus teaches us how to pray, we should listen (see Matt. 6:9–13 and Luke 11:2–4). Jesus teaches us the proper dispositions we should have in prayer and the kinds of things we should ask for. Memorizing and reciting this prayer is beneficial, but Jesus also expects that we will elaborate on the prayer (e.g., confessing specific sins, not merely sins in general).

ACTS

A popular model of prayer is the acronym ACTS, which stands for adoration, confession, thanksgiving, and supplication. While this is not a biblically mandated model of prayer, it provides a structure that reminds us of who God is (adoration) and our need for His forgiving grace (confession). Because God has promised forgiveness through His Son, we respond to this assurance (with thanksgiving). And finally, we bring our requests to Him (supplication). There are several other structuring devices that you might find helpful such as PRAY: praise, repent, ask, yield.

CONCENTRIC CIRCLES

This is a practical way to organize your prayer requests, whether you are praying privately or with others. Begin by praying for yourself, then your immediate family, then your church, then your community, and then the world. The idea is that you are asking God to act in various spheres of your life. The "circles" can be adjusted to fit the needs of your prayer time.

Conclusion

Prayer is an expression of faith. In prayer, Christians acknowledge that the Triune God hears and responds to the prayers of believers. It is the way that the children of God relate to God the Father through the work of God the Son in the intercession of God the Spirit. It is our privilege as children of God. Nevertheless, most Christians report that they wish they prayed more often. I resonate with that sentiment. Prayer, like anything that is important, must have priority. Here is the encouraging thing. Prayer tends to build on itself. The hardest part of having a prayer-shaped life is starting. When you experience the joy of communing with God, see Him shape your heart, and witness His answers to prayer, your desire for prayer will increase.

Reflection Questions

1. How might one's prayer life reflect his or her view of God?
2. What is one aspect of prayer that you wish were truer of your life (e.g., consistency, perseverance, joy, etc.)? What is one thing you can do to grow in this area? Who could help you grow?
3. How can you use the Bible to inform and shape your prayers?
4. Which of the methods for stronger prayer could you implement this week?

4

Church

Why does the church matter?

I (Trent) was a committed and maturing Christian when I went to college. The disciplines described in the previous two chapters (Bible reading and prayer) were true of me. But I failed miserably in my engagement with the church, and I paid a price for this neglect. I didn't stop attending church altogether because I thought Christians should attend church. I went on Sundays, but I did not contribute meaningfully to the church, nor did I allow the church to shape me meaningfully. I led campus ministries, and I led Bible studies. In some ways, I thought the church might slow me down in my discipleship and evangelism of others. The church was (and is) made up of people different from me. They had different preferences in music. I also arrogantly thought that most people did not want to think as deeply about doctrine as I did. I did not see what the church had to offer me, and I was already very engaged in other ministries.

You might have expected that someone who fancied himself as a deep thinker would have changed his mind when he read the Bible on his own. You might have thought that I read passages like Hebrews 10:25 and realized that my Christian walk was not in step with the Bible. Or you might have assumed that I read 1 Corinthians 12 and realized that God had designed me to serve and be served in the church. Or you might have anticipated that I read almost any book from church history and realized that there is a consistent pattern of Christians engaging with the church.

But my life is a cautionary tale of proud self-sufficiency leading to a blindness of the heart. The "aha moment" came for me when I wanted to pursue marriage and then also in the early years of marriage. I began to realize how much I had to learn and from whom I had to learn it. That Christian in the church who liked different music from me and was not eager to debate an arcane theological point had been married happily for decades. He was raising godly children. He was respected for his godly character. He was the embodiment of biblical wisdom, and in many ways, I was embodying foolishness. I NEEDED THE CHURCH. The people of the church could have reacted with skepticism to this young, not-too-humble Christian who had not shown that he cared about the church. Instead, the church embraced me. And as I embraced the church, I learned the church needed me as well. That mutual need and fulfillment should have been predictable since God designed it that way.

For most of Christian history, the natural impulse for someone committed to Jesus Christ was to commit to a local church. Only recently has an anti-institutionalism impulse, an issue much broader than the church, taken root among Christians. When you meet "lone ranger Christians" and ask them why they do not engage in church, they usually counter with, "Why should I engage in the local church?" To their minds, the default position is not to engage the church. They might be rejecting the church due to some past or present hurt by the church. They might be rejecting the church due to a suspicion of institutions. They might be rejecting the church due to a preference for making their own way in the world. Or they might simply be unaware of the role the church should have in their lives. Whatever the reason for this outlook, neglecting the church surely falls short of the command to love one another. So what is the church, and what role does it have in the Christian life?

Is the church global or local?

When the Bible describes the church, it can mean believers in all times and places who have trusted in Jesus Christ for salvation. That is, everyone who is a Christian is part of the universal church. Paul describes the universal church as a group of people purchased by the blood of Christ. "And he is the head of the body, the church. He is the beginning, the firstborn from the dead, that in everything he might be preeminent. For in him all the fullness of God was pleased to dwell, and through him to reconcile to himself all things, whether on earth or in heaven, making peace by the blood of his cross" (Col. 1:18–20). Jesus Christ is the head over the church which He redeemed through His death on the cross and His resurrection. Jesus also promises that this universal organization will ultimately be victorious over evil: "…I will build my church, and the gates of hell shall not prevail against it" (Matt. 16:18).

But "church" can also be a plural noun, "churches", for groups that exist in multiple locations (e.g., Acts 11:2; 13:1; 16:5) with local leadership (e.g., 1 Tim. 3:1–7; Titus 1:5–9; James 5:14; 1 Pet. 5:1–5). For example, Paul writes to the church at Corinth: "To the church of God that is in Corinth, to those sanctified in Christ Jesus, called to be saints together with all those who in every place call upon the name of our Lord Jesus Christ, both their Lord and ours…" (1 Cor. 1:2). It is in these multiple local churches that the singular universal church is seen and performs ministry in the world. So by virtue of believing in Jesus, we are a part of the universal church, but there is action that we must take to be a part of a local church. Two questions are important. What is a local church? And why should I commit to a local church?

What is the local church?

The first thing to note when defining the local church is the adjective "local." This adjective is a distinction from the term "universal," so that the local church is one among many groups of people who are a part of the single universal church.

The authors of the New Testament do not provide a dictionary definition of what a local church is. Instead, they use various analogies or pictures to communicate what the church is. Let's look at three descriptions: the people of God, body, and flock.

CHURCH AS THE PEOPLE OF GOD

To describe the nature of the church, the New Testament draws on the Old Testament description of the people of God. The image of the church as the people of God emphasizes the continuity of Christians with the Old Testament people of God. One New Testament text that describes the church as the people of God is 1 Peter 2. Peter writes to a group of believers who are enduring persecution. He encourages them to be holy and remain faithful in these difficult times. He challenges them to stand firm in the faith, and he reminds them of their identity in Christ. Peter's description of the church is remarkable in its analogy: "But you are a chosen race, a royal priesthood, a holy nation, a people for his own possession, that you may proclaim the excellencies of him who called you out of darkness into his marvelous light. Once you were not a people, but now you are God's people; once you had not received mercy, but now you have received mercy" (1 Pet. 2:9–10). The church is a "chosen race" and a "holy nation," although not in the sense of ethnic uniformity since Christians are from all peoples; rather, it is a contrast with the Old Covenant made with the descendants of Abraham. Christians are "royal priests" in the sense that they have the royal inheritance of the kingdom of God. They function as priests in the world to represent God to the people. And the exclamation point is on the church as the people of God. Christians are those who "have received mercy" through the work of Jesus Christ. Their fundamental identity is that they believe in Jesus Christ. And this identity changes their relationship with others. They now have a group identity as the people of God. The Bible can also describe this relationship as the family of God. We have a relationship with the Father through the Son, and thereby we have relationships with other children of God.

CHURCH AS BODY

Using the analogy of a human body, Paul communicates that the church is a unit formed of diverse parts. Each of the parts must perform its function if the whole is to perform its function. In the church, each member is dependent on the other members. Paul states rhetorically: "For the body does not consist of one member but of many. If the foot should say, 'Because I am not a hand, I do not belong to the body,' that would not make it any less a part of the body" (1 Cor. 12:14–15). When Paul uses the imagery of the body in 1 Corinthians 12 and Romans 12, he emphasizes our unity and interdependence rather than our diversity—diversity is taken for granted. While we might like to think of ourselves as self-sufficient and independent, the Bible describes us as dependent on one another in the church. Interdependence is God's good design: "God arranged the members in the body, each one of them, as he chose" (1 Cor. 12:18). The goal of this interdependent relationship is that "the members may have the same care for one another" (1 Cor. 12:25). If we are to engage the local church rightly, we must avoid the errors of jealousy (12:14–20) and self-sufficiency (14:21–26). We must serve one another and be served—those are the needs with which God designed us.

CHURCH AS FLOCK

Another image that the Bible uses to communicate something about the church is that of a "flock." Many of us have not spent considerable time around flocks, but the image can nevertheless resonate with us. Peter addresses the leaders, also called pastors or elders, of a local church and charges them to "shepherd the flock of God that is among you, exercising oversight, not under compulsion, but willingly, as God would have you; not for shameful gain, but eagerly; not domineering over those in your charge, but being examples to the flock" (1 Pet. 5:2–3). The existence and importance of leadership is taken for granted. Peter does not try to argue for leadership; he merely explains the way leadership should be conducted.

Pastors are like shepherds who care for the flock of God. They are representatives of the chief Shepherd, Christ, and as such they must care for the flock like He does (1 Pet. 5:4). But what does it mean for a local church to be a flock? Like the image of the body, the image of a flock communicates that there are many individuals (sheep or Christians) who make up one whole (flock or local church). What does it take for individual Christians to receive leadership and love one another? Peter's answer is simple, humility. "Clothe yourselves, all of you, with humility toward one another, for 'God opposes the proud but gives grace to the humble'" (1 Pet. 5:5). Failure to commit seriously to others in a local church or failure to receive spiritual leadership from local church pastors is a mark of spiritual pride. It is a mark of rejecting God's good design for the Christian life.

Why should I commit to a local church?

Think back to the opening example when a lone ranger Christian asks why he should join a church. Why should a person join himself or herself to a local Bible-believing and gospel-preaching church? There are several answers, but these brief categories will communicate the loving intent of the Bible's commands. Here are some reasons to commit to the local church:

- COMMUNITY...because God created you for community. God created humans to be relational, and a theme that runs throughout the Bible is that God's people gather together in worshipping communities.
- JESUS' EXAMPLE...because you follow a savior who modeled community. The incarnation is remarkable because God the Son assumed human nature to live with us (John 1:14)—Jesus is Immanuel, God with us (Matt. 1:23). And as Jesus lived with humanity, He had community with the 3, 12, 72, 5,000, etc. He didn't isolate Himself.

Church

- OBEDIENCE...because God commands you to commit to the church. The pattern of Christians in the New Testament is that they gather in churches, and it is also an explicit command (e.g., 1 Pet. 5:1–5; Heb. 13:17).
- SPIRITUAL GROWTH...because you need others to grow in holiness and others need you. Christians have a role and responsibility for other Christians' growth in Christ. Hebrews 3:12 warns against Christians having an unbelieving heart, and then gives, as the antidote, the ministry of other believers.
- SPIRITUAL GIFTS...because you need others to use your spiritual gifts. The text we looked at above, 1 Corinthians 12, explains the importance of using your gifts for the ministry to the body. Your gifts are designed to be used for the good of others, and you need others to use those gifts.
- MISSION...because you need others to expand in mission. While all Christians share the gospel, one function of the church is to cooperate for increased missional impact and discipleship.[1]
- GOD'S GLORY...because you are committed to the glory of God. God's plan is to be glorified by being demonstrated to be a worldwide God. He is calling to Himself a people from every tongue, tribe, and nation (Matt. 28:18–20; Rev. 5:9–10). And His glory is on display in the world presently as people from diverse backgrounds gather together for the sole unifying reason of their belief in Jesus Christ.

Conclusion

---

1. Here's one pastor's explanation of the significance of the church for ministry and mission: "The local church – this Father-designed, Jesus-authorized, and Spirit-gifted body – is far better equipped to undertake the work of discipling believers than simply you and your one friend. Jesus does not promise that you and your one friend will defeat the gates of hell. He promises that the church will do this. You cannot recognize yourself as gifted and called to teach God's Word, or to baptize and administer the Lord's Supper, like a local church is so authorized" (Mark Dever, *Discipling: How to Help Others Follow Jesus* [Wheaton, IL: Crossway, 2016], 69).

It turns out the "lone ranger" Christian approach falls flat in many ways. What most people who choose this path do not see is that they are losing out on the opportunity for joy. Meaningful investment in a local church is participation in something God is building. The church is where God corporately works in and through His people. The church is the God-designed entity to bring the good news of salvation to the world—it has His promise that its mission will not fail. The church also shepherds your soul toward holiness and hope.

While I made some sinful missteps in college, I want you to know that the church is now precious to me. I love my fellow church members deeply. We have done evangelism and discipleship together. We have wept together and rejoiced together. There have been hard times, and there have been really good times. They are my family. And the great thing about a well-functioning family is that the members of the family love one another and are always for the others' good. My prayer for you is that you would commit to a local church and experience the joy and growth that come from being part of God's family.

Reflection Questions

1. What benefits might you experience from serious commitment to a local church?
2. What benefit might you be able to contribute to a local church?
3. What is more likely to keep you from serious engagement with the local church: feelings of jealousy or feelings of self-sufficiency?
4. What steps can you take now to ensure your college experience includes committing to a church near your campus?

5

Character

Who should I become?

How do I become the right kind of person?

Think about the people in your life who have impacted you the most. This list could be those who have positively affected you or others who have left scars. What is it about the people on that list that brings them to mind today? Chances are good that the impact tracks back to their character. The people who positively shape us are characterized by patience, acceptance, inspiration, encouragement, steadfastness, courage, faith, above all by love. The people who impact us negatively tend to be impatient, angry, inconsistent, manipulative, cowardly, above all self-centered. We instinctively and emotionally affirm or reject the character of the person at the mere memory of them. Identifying the positive and negative influences in our lives will demonstrate the value of personal character.

Our experiences illustrate the value of character, and they touch on something quite profound. God cares about our character. In our gravity toward self-importance, we often think the things we do are the most important things about us in God's eyes. God cares foremost about who we *are* and then what we *do* flows from our character. Sometimes, we think we are impressing God by our performance before Him. In contrast, God says that He is far more interested in right hearts rather than religious performance: "All these things my hand has made, and so all these things came to be, declares the Lord. But this is the one to whom I will look: he who is humble and contrite in spirit and trembles at my word" (Isa. 66:2).

Sometimes, we compare ourselves with other people and then think God's perspective is decided by how gifted, lovable, attractive, or personable we are. God says He is far more interested in inward character than external charm: "But the Lord said to Samuel, 'Do not look on his appearance or on the height of his stature, because I have rejected him. For the Lord sees not as man sees: man looks on the outward appearance, but the Lord looks on the heart'" (1 Sam. 16:7).

Sometimes, we measure our success by how highly others esteem our talents and abilities. The Apostle Paul was familiar with this temptation when faced by others claiming to be apostles who comparatively looked more outwardly impressive. Through Paul, God says He is far more interested in genuine substance than worldly winners: "We are not commending ourselves to you again but giving you cause to boast about us, so that you may be able to answer those who boast about outward appearance and not about what is in the heart" (2 Cor. 5:12).

Our character is indisputably valuable, both in our experience and in God's perspective. The questions are, what character should we aim to build and how should we reach it?

What character should I seek to build?

The Bible provides a broad and beautiful picture of honorable character. Imagine a panoramic vista in the western United States that includes in one view the variety of an expansive desert, blue skies, and mountains in the distance. The Bible provides a comprehensive picture of the beauty God designed humanity to express. We will summarize a few facets below. Let's look at Psalm 15 as our guide. This song in God's Word is structured as a short question, a long answer, and a strong assurance.

Character

> O Lord, who shall sojourn in your tent?
>> Who shall dwell on your holy hill?
> He who walks blamelessly and does what is right
>> and speaks truth in his heart;
> who does not slander with his tongue
>> and does no evil to his neighbor,
>>> nor takes up a reproach against his friend;
> in whose eyes a vile person is despised,
>> but who honors those who fear the Lord;
> who swears to his own hurt and does not change;
> who does not put out his money at interest
>> and does not take a bribe against the innocent.
> He who does these things shall never be moved.

The Psalm begins with the question, "Who can dwell in God's presence?" This question is the Psalmist's way of asking the question we raised above. What does God value? Who does He esteem? Is it external flash, online influencers, and the most popular on the scene? Who will He permit to enjoy the good things of His presence? The fact that the author of this song begins with this question shows a stroke of humility right out of the gate. There is no assumption that anyone can define their own way into fellowship with God. Instead, God is the Holy one, and those rightly identified as His worshipers draw near to His presence.

The answer reveals the kind of character possessed by a true worshiper of God. Remember that performance in these traits does not earn salvation (see chapter 1 on the gospel for clarification). Instead, these character traits result from God's work and are the hallmarks of a true worshiper.

WALKS BLAMELESSLY

The person who walks blamelessly is consistent in each life circumstance. No person is perfect, but the blameless person can say without hypocrisy that his typical way of life is as God desires it to be, whether in public or in private. There are no clear and obvious mismatches between how he acts in specific settings and who he claims to be. When he does fail, he acknowledges it to God and the appropriate people, and then strives forward in the renewed pursuit of consistency.

SPEAKS THE TRUTH

A person of character is conscientiously honest and speaks truthfully in her dealings. When there are moments where she could benefit personally by cutting the truth in half, she simply states the truth. Speaking truth starts with words and extends into every facet of life. Honesty in academic work, completing the full drill when the coach is not looking in sports practice, and accuracy on the time clock at work are all lived examples of truthfulness. Truthfulness in all her dealings starts in a heart that knows the truth and knows it is always worth choosing God's way.

DOES NOT SLANDER

Words build up, and words tear down. Words bring life to the souls of our friends, or words have the power to damage people God cares about. Making false and damaging statements about a person not only inflicts emotional pain on someone, but it treats people as though they are not valued for who they are. The non-believing world is characterized by a willingness to speak untruth about another person if it provides personal benefit to the speaker. In contrast, the standard God calls us to follow is building one another up, strengthening each other, and giving life with our words. This applies to words launched by a keyboard into digital space just as much as words said in person.

DOES NO EVIL TO NEIGHBOR OR REPROACH TO A FRIEND

Avoiding evil toward your neighbor may seem like an obvious and low bar of conduct. But, when the standard is building up others because they are my neighbor, the standard is raised. Is my attitude charitable and thinking the best about others? Do I go out of my way to serve others in a way that costs me time and money? Do I live in a way that people are better, strengthened, and encouraged because they happen to be in my proximity?

HONORS WHAT GOD HONORS

A person of character knows when and how to love a neighbor and friend truly, but this charity is not done at the expense of affirming what God does not affirm. Psalm 15 goes so far to say that a person of character will grow to hate what God hates, and he will love what God loves. There is no legitimate reason to envy what a person gains by sinful means. The person of character rests securely in knowing even worldly treasures, satisfactions, and acceptance may pass us by on the way to higher glories in God's design. Godly character laments and pities those who eat mudpies over a feast of the finest foods. Conversely, the person of character esteems those who manifest godliness and pursues fellowship with such people.

LIVES GENEROUSLY

A person of generous character contrasts with a person who acts selfishly toward others for financial gain. A woman of character sticks with her word even when following through on a promise is costly in a way she did not anticipate. A man of character does not focus on his gain from others. In Israelite society, loaning money at interest was a way of extorting and gaining from someone else's challenging circumstances. This was an expression of self-focus rather than generosity to those in need. Another expression of self-gain was taking bribes and showing partiality. Seeking benefit from one person or group would result in disregard for another person or group. Leveraging cliques and friendships in ways that bestow selective acceptance fits this pattern. Good character is impartially generous and caring for all people. Money is not the only application. Social status, time, proximity, and relationship can manifest the same favoritism.

Psalm 15 started with a question and gave an answer summarized in these six character qualities. The song ends with a strong assurance. You may have a sense that choosing this sort of character is costly. It may change relationships. It might result in not climbing the ladder at work, on a team, or in your circle of friends. Every one of us feels the pressure to compromise character to attain something that appears beneficial. That is why the song ends with a strong assurance. That assurance is that the person of character "will not be moved." That is a poetic way of saying the young man who chooses godly character over personal gain will not lose ultimately. The young woman who speaks with virtue rather than tearing down another to elevate herself will not be left behind. There may be a cost in worldly terms, but the assurance is that the Lord always sees and honors faithfulness. He always knows when we choose His way. He is always on our side when we anchor our lives in His established virtues. You may lose the world, but you will gain God.

Remember the image of a panoramic landscape full of beauty at every glimpse? The description above is but one part of a vast picture of character provided in the Bible. You can explore other parts of the vista in the book of Proverbs; Psalm 1; Galatians 5:22–25; Romans 5:1–5; Philippians 4:8–9; Titus 2:7–8; and 2 Peter 1:5–11.

How do I grow in my character?

There is one more aspect of character to highlight. Developing character requires self-control and putting truth into action. Habits driven by deferring gratification and choosing what is right over personal gain are essential. At the same time, character does not amount to a list of duties performed to achieve righteousness. Law-keeping does not produce heart-level righteousness. An external commitment to behavior is not the sum of the Christian way of life. Great religious performance can still be far from a heart of true righteousness, as evidenced by the Pharisees in Jesus' ministry. To get character right, we need to explore two questions. How should we pursue character? What do we do when we fail in our character?

How should we pursue character?

Christian character recognizes that true transformation is the work of God and progresses from the inside out. The message of the gospel is not that people lacking character must conform themselves to God's way so that God will accept them. The gospel is that God accepts those who lack character based on Christ's work and, in the process, works within them to make their character more like His. Paul describes this as the fruit of the Spirit (Gal. 5:22–23). Love, joy, peace, patience, kindness, goodness, and self-control are attributes of God. These attributes become increasingly clear where God dwells, transforming whoever He touches. Through faith in Christ, God dwells within each believer, and so He is bringing transformation to a Christian's character to match His character.

Yet it is also our responsibility to "walk in the Spirit." Walking is an analogy that conveys step-by-step decisions. Walking involves placing your feet progressively in place after place to pursue a direction. Your step-by-step decisions take you in one direction as opposed to many other directions you could go. Walking in the Spirit is a daily, even moment by moment, habit of knowing and choosing God's ways. This daily walk represents our human decisions to welcome God's work of bringing inward transformation that manifests in outward character. We pursue character by living in ongoing union with Christ, where genuine transformation is imparted, and by disciplining ourselves for godliness in pursuit of godly character. Focus on God's work to change you while not falling into passivity. Likewise, give wholehearted attention to spiritual disciplines, fighting sin, and forming patterns of good character while not falling into self-driven effort.

What do we do when we fail in our character?

Sometimes, we fail because we are sinners still on a journey toward Christlikeness. When we fail in character, the Bible provides a clear guide for what to do next. Proverbs 28:13 tells us there are two steps to take: "Whoever conceals his transgressions will not prosper, but he who confesses and forsakes them will obtain mercy."

First, we confess. Humbly acknowledge before God and to the people our sin impacted, that we have failed in character. Dressing it up, softening the narrative, rationalizing, or minimizing the significance is unproductive. God already knows, and often, other people will come to know (if they do not already) our character inadequacies. Readily confess and find compassion rather than hide and experience ongoing friction in conscience and relationships.

Second, we forsake our sin. Forsaking means turning away, leaving behind, and pursuing a different direction. Is your failure of character related to truthfulness? Confess and then set a course away from dishonesty and toward truthfulness. A significant facet of pursuing a new course is surrounding yourself with people of character who have strengths in the same area in which you have weaknesses. Do you struggle with your words about other people? Intentionally surround yourself with people who are strong at encouraging others. Along the way, fill your mind with Scripture as the means the Holy Spirit has provided to change us (2 Tim. 3:16-17).

This process of confessing and forsaking is what Christians call "repentance." Repentance is typically uncomfortable but recognizes the promise inherent at the end of the Proverb above. Repentance is the pathway that leads to mercy. God is eager for us to turn to Him in our failures as He continues conforming us to Christlikeness.

Conclusion

Reverse the question from the introduction of this chapter. You know who has impacted you the most based on their character. When other people think about your character, what do you want them to associate with their experience with you? The good news is your choice to pursue godly character glorifies God and can influence others. Do you desire to impact others? Dedicate yourself to developing your character. By God's grace, you can grow to be an extraordinary influence on those around you.

Reflection Questions:

1. What character qualities do you most value in other people?
2. What are your character strengths and weaknesses? Could you list 4–5 of each?
3. Are there instances of character failure you need to confess and forsake? If so, what is your next step?
4. What steps can you take to address your character weaknesses?

Part 2

Christian Vocation

6

Life Purpose

What is the Christian vocation?

My family (Jon) loves outdoor adventures, particularly hiking. Reading trail maps is a necessary skill to develop for navigating the wilderness. In an age of beautifully designed turn-by-turn navigation on our vehicle dashboards, following a trail map's minimal representation of paths and topography is no longer intuitive. The advantage of a trail map is that it shows you the big picture and orients your current steps to the larger purpose of your expedition. Humanity is hardwired to look for the trail map of life. What is my purpose, and where should I go on my life path?

The word "vocation" is likely not in your everyday vocabulary. Yet, it has a rich history of communicating the significance of the pursuits we have in life and how those pursuits fit on the trail map of God's purposes for you. "Vocation" comes from Latin and indicates a "calling or summons." That calling is a combination of the internal desires about what you are convinced you should do with your life and the external circumstances that are inherently your "summons" to specific responsibilities. Every person has a vocation and, in reality, multiple vocations.

There are multiple roles any person bears at the intersection of what you are called to do, what you are equipped to do, and what you bear responsibility to steward in faithfulness. The fact that you are reading this book in preparation for college indicates that you probably have significant freedom in determining what vocations you will pursue in life. For your career, will you pursue engineering or education? Relationally, will you pursue marriage and family or singleness? In your church community, where will you serve and with whom? In your local community, will you embrace formal responsibility on a board or pursue informal relational connections? Each of these is an example of choice in pursuing the various vocations of life. Before you can make decisions about questions like these, you need to understand the expedition you are on. That brings us back to the trail map. God's trail map orients all our roles and provides their purpose.

What is the backdrop of vocation?

Getting to the root of our purpose requires starting at the beginning. Who we are and how we got here reveals an immense amount about our life purpose. The fact that God created us and we are His creation is the compass on the map that orients everything else. We may not often realize it, but our thinking about how we got here supplies our answer for why we are here. When there is no apparent purposefulness for how we got here, the inevitable and consistent conclusion is that there is no purpose for why we are here. In contrast, if we are here for another, that defines our purpose. So, we need to reckon with the question, "Why did God create?"

WHY DID GOD CREATE US?

There are a few popular *wrong* answers to this question, including the following:

- God needed someone for a relationship.
- God needed an outlet for His attributes to be demonstrated.
- God needed humanity to give Him glory (as though He lacked something). As some state less nobly, God is a selfish monster who needs humanity to fulfill His inward cravings for attention.

- We don't know why God created, but all we know is He provides a place for humanity to dwell in mortality and prove themselves worthy, through keeping the commandments, to return to the presence of God from whence they came.

According to the Scriptures, there is only one answer for why God created (Isa. 43:7; Rom. 11:36). God created the world to glorify Himself. How is this different from the wrong answers above, which all assume God needed something from outside of Himself (e.g., glory, love, relationship, or something to do)? The difference lies in what it means for God to glorify Himself and what humanity was given in creation. God does not need validation, love, or a relationship outside of Himself. He is entirely sufficient and infinitely complete within Himself. God is the perfection of His attributes as Father, Son, and Holy Spirit. God is an infinitely flowing fountain of the most beautiful and excellent attributes we could ever summon to our mind about Him.

God's glorification of Himself through creation is not about what God needs but how He is glorified in giving to humanity. Specifically, God created the world to dwell among worshipers who are satisfied in knowing Him. Through sharing His eternal relationship of Father, Son, and Holy Spirit with human beings created in His image, God provides the fullness of satisfaction for humanity and gains glory for Himself.

I claimed that creation provides the orientation for the entire trail map of decisions about human vocation. How is that the case? God's purpose in creation is to glorify Himself by dwelling among satisfied worshipers. Therefore, the purpose of God's people is to worship God by living in the satisfaction of knowing Him. One historic document of the church (Westminster Shorter Catechism) famously communicates this orienting reality of human purpose in the first question:

Q: What is the chief end of man?

A: Man's chief end is to glorify God and enjoy Him forever.

Our ultimate purpose is to dwell with God and enjoy fellowship with Him. 1 Corinthians 10:31 tells us that whatever we do in everyday life can be done to the glory of God. We've established the compass and scale of the trail map for life. Now, let's start understanding the topographical features and how to hike the trails.

How do you find your vocations?

Life is not just one thing. There are layers and multiple roles you fill at any time. Connecting the grand purpose of life to everyday life requires zooming in at a few stages. The first of these stages is to understand the primary calling on all Christians. Remember, vocation is a calling defined by our internal ambitions and external circumstances. Some of our vocations are chosen, some result inevitably from our choices, and others are chosen for us. Our primary calling is determined from outside of us and is universal to all Christians.

PRIMARY VOCATION

Glorifying God in all things may sound vague, but it translates to some everyday pursuits God desires for everyone. These pursuits can be summarized in the word "discipleship." The gospel message of Jesus Christ calls us to follow Him in faith. Following the confession of faith in Christ and our sinfulness, we commence a lifelong journey of learning from and living for Jesus. Our journey of being Jesus' disciples includes committing to other disciples in a church community. Along the way, there are many manifestations of following Jesus. We read the Bible to know Him; we persevere through suffering; we endure opposition; we encourage one another; we fellowship with God in prayer; we confess sin to one another; and many other activities of the Christian life. In addition to pursuing Jesus, we actively pursue the commission Jesus gave His church to be and make disciples. The primary vocation of all followers of Christ in this world is to follow Jesus in everyday life faithfully and personally make disciples.

SECONDARY VOCATIONS

This talk of primary calling is spiritual sounding, but what about all the time and energy we must spend on things that are not our primary calling? This is where the secondary callings of life enter the picture. A secondary calling is how we use our gifts and opportunities to serve God and others. Examples of secondary callings are:

- Educating others and developing people
- Meeting human needs
- Ensuring safe environments for society
- Meeting the physical needs of the ill and fostering health and healing
- Raising the next generation
- Enabling human communication and creative production
- Conveying beauty and communicating ideas creatively
- Preaching the Bible and shepherding a church

The list could go on. The point is that most roles we fill in life can be a means to serve God and other people. Secondary callings provide the overarching themes for what motivates our work. There is inevitably an element of personal desire and inherent ability to fill such a role. God is at work through various vocations, so it is no wonder He has designed us to have strong desires and skills in particular ways of serving Him and no desires and abilities in other ways.

At the same time, contrary to the message of our society, your vocation(s) are not purely self-chosen. We indeed live in a time when we have the most freedom to decide what we want to do with our lives according to our desires. At the same time, our vocations are not always determined by an internal, passionate desire. Internal desire is not an explicit declaration of how to not waste your life. Sometimes, calling comes through external circumstances. Limited educational opportunities, economic resources, personal health, or lack of family support can impact our options. In this sense, the goal for identifying our secondary calling is not solely to decide what we are passionate about. It is impossible to be passionate about even the most attractive interests forever. Overblown emphasis on passion hints at an idolatry of work, whereby our careers provide meaning and significance that can only be found in Christ alone. Determine your secondary calling with the balance of how you desire to serve the Lord, the abilities you can utilize, and the counsel of wise people regarding how you can impact the world.

JOBS, CAREERS, AND ROLES

There is one final category downstream from vocation. We often start with jobs and careers as the definition of life's purpose. In the Christian framing, the case is the opposite. A job is a practical way to serve God and the world. A career is a string of jobs with a common theme that serves God and the world. Roles are non-paid – yet still critically important – vocational manifestations like a stay-at-home mom or volunteer pastor in your church.

Whether blue-collar or white-collar, highly paid or volunteer, owner or employee, part-time or full-time – all jobs, careers, and roles are meant to play out your primary and secondary vocational responsibilities as the means for glorifying God. Rather than providing life purpose, careers serve life's ultimate purpose. Secondary callings can manifest themselves in various jobs, careers, and roles. The following chart demonstrates the variety of ways secondary callings can be manifested.

Secondary Calling	Example Jobs, Careers, and Roles
Educating others and developing people	School teacher, homeschooling mom, professor
Meeting human needs	Social worker, counselor, non-profit leader, local church deacon
Ensuring safe environments for society	Engineer, police officer, sanitation worker
Meeting the physical needs of the ill and facilitating healing	Nurse, doctor, physical therapist
Raising the next generation	Parent, grandparent, foster care
Enabling human communication and creative production	Software engineer, IT manager, supply chain manager, ESL teacher
Conveying beauty and communicating ideas creatively	Artist, writer, graphic designer
Teaching the Bible and shepherding a church	Pastor, youth pastor, lay elder

Conclusion

In summary, the Christian vocation is ordered by the graphic below. At the top of the diagram, our pursuits should be ordered by God's ultimate purpose for humanity. While this might seem like a vague starting point, committing to live for God's purposes is essential for making wise decisions. From there, the focal points narrow down to what you will do for a job. While the priorities at the top of the diagram influence the decisions in the bottom boxes, our daily activities in the boxes at the bottom glorify God because they serve the ultimate purposes above them.

The trail map is in your hands. It will not tell you which trails you should hike. At least with clarity about the orientation of the map, the basic topography, and what trails are available to you, you can make informed decisions. Similarly, the basics of Christian vocation help us understand the purpose of humanity, our purpose as Christians, and how our choices about daily responsibilities connect to God's grand plan. With the trail map for life in front of you, explore confidently.

The Christian Vocation

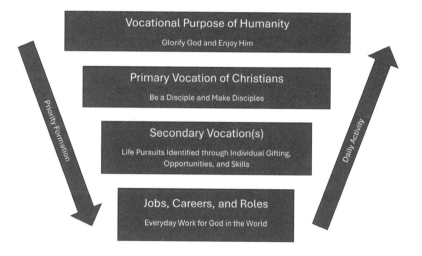

Life Purpose

Reflection Questions

1. How do you think humanity's ultimate purpose should influence how you think about everyday pursuits like education, a career, and family?
2. In what ways are you pursuing your primary vocation of growing as a disciple and making disciples of other people?
3. What do you currently think your secondary vocation is? Write out the possibilities based on your desires, circumstances, and external feedback from people you trust.
4. What are the practical steps of faithfulness you should take in your current jobs and roles to live out your secondary vocation well?

7

Work

Is work a good thing?

"Find something you're passionate about, and you'll never work a day in your life," so the mantra goes. There is something that is appealing in this statement—we would all love to devote most of our time to things we love to do. Genuinely loving what we do would make doing tasks day in and day out much easier. It would solve the problem of motivation. The idea is that we would be internally and sustainably motivated by our passions.

Yet there's a catch—our passions tend to change. For some of us, our passions change fairly rapidly. If we are motivated to work merely because we are passionate about the topic, what will we do when we are no longer passionate? Do we change jobs or emphases within jobs? Most people, even those who might be characterized by a passion for their work, have times in which their motivation wanes. Nevertheless, what they're doing might still be valuable and worth doing. Additionally, there are people who hate preparing for a job that they will ultimately love, and they have to work to get to the goal of the job. Let's also recognize that very few people in the history of the world have had the privilege of choosing what they would do occupationally. For most people in the world, both past and present, circumstances dictated what they would do for work, regardless of their passion for it.

So, there are some problems with the mantra of pursuing your passion. It applies to only a very, very small percentage of the population. And it might keep us from doing things that are truly good and about which we might truly have currently undiscovered passions.

Are there any theological problems with this mantra? Yes, there are theological problems with this statement. It assumes that work is a bad thing. The goal is to "never work a day." We want to play and are willing to work so long as our work is more like play that we would not even call it work.

Consider the Apostle Paul's counsel to a church: "But we urge you, brothers, to do this [i.e., love one another] more and more, and to aspire to live quietly, and to mind your own affairs, and to work with your hands, as we instructed you, so that you may walk properly before outsiders and be dependent on no one" (1 Thess. 4:10–12). Paul's instructions are that Christians work diligently as a testimony to their faith in Christ.

Or consider Paul's instructions about how someone should live out their new identity in Christ: "Let the thief no longer steal, but rather let him labor, doing honest work with his own hands, so that he may have something to share with anyone in need" (Eph. 4:28). Part of being a new creation in Christ is that a Christian must work diligently to help others.

One thing that Paul does not talk about is our passion for work. But since this is an argument from silence, let's see what the Bible says about work.

How does the Bible present work?

In the biblical storyline, work is part of God's good, created order. The Bible begins with God working effortlessly (Gen. 1–2). He creates marvelously by speaking. So, the first image of God that the Bible presents is one of a dynamic, active, and effective God. God works. Just as the Bible presents God working, so the humans created in His image are expected to work. Humanity is entrusted with tasks related to the world (e.g., having dominion and subduing, collecting food)

Work

and to family (e.g., being fruitful and multiplying). Eden is a prototypical sanctuary of life with God, so tending the garden is a service in the sanctuary; thus, Adam's work is his worship. While Adam's work requires effort, his work is effective, joy-filled, and worshipful. In Eden, God's provision of food for Adam and Eve, while requiring effort and work, was abundant and joy-filled.

The tragic irony of the Garden is that Satan tempts Eve to doubt God's provision (Gen. 3:1–5), and as a result, the means of provision is frustrated greatly. In part, God's punishment of Adam and Eve is to frustrate their work (Gen. 3:17–19). Outside of Eden, it is a struggle to make crops grow. It is a struggle to make ends meet. In the Garden of Eden, work was inherently good because it was service to God and worship. Outside of Eden, work can be divorced from worship, and people can work for foolish or futile goals. Work divorced from worship is futile and meaningless because it is robbed of its greater, God-oriented purpose. The author of Ecclesiastes describes the meaninglessness of life and work that are not oriented toward the glory of God: "So I hated life, because what is done under the sun was grievous to me, for all is vanity and a striving after wind" (2:17).

Even while work after the Fall can be unproductive and not oriented toward worship, people are expected to work. The Bible assumes that people will work. And God's blessing is often portrayed in how He blesses their work. Through his work, Joseph saves nations and God's people (Gen. 41–47). Ruth's diligence in work is praised as she provides for Naomi (Ruth 1–2). Daniel's work is good even though it was rendered to a pagan king. Nehemiah's wise rule and construction of the wall are held out as examples of wisdom and diligence. While not explicit on every page of Scripture, the underlying assumption is that God's people will work diligently. The instructions for a sabbath rest assume that there will be toil. Rest only makes sense when work is present.

On this side of Eden, work is hard, frustrating, and often ineffective. We toil and do not always produce. Because work is a universal human experience, it becomes an effective way to communicate salvation. Recognizing that people cannot work themselves into a right relationship with God, Jesus says, "Come to me, all who labor and are heavy laden, and I will give you rest" (Matt. 11:28). Those who recognize the insufficiency of their work to be in a right relationship with God are in a place to relate to Him by faith in the work that Jesus Christ has done: "And to the one who does not work but believes in him who justifies the ungodly, his faith is counted as righteousness" (Rom. 4:5). And God's work does not stop by providing salvation, He continues to be active in our Christian growth, "it is God who works in you, both to will and to work for his good pleasure" (Phil. 2:13). Salvation is about the work of God in us, and thus, work is a manner in which we "image" God in the world.

Will there be work in heaven? If there is work, it will look different from what it does today. It will not be frustrated or frustrating. It will not be divorced from worship. At least we can say that we will work in the sense of worshipping (Rev. 21–22), and that we will reign (Rev. 5:10). The Bible begins with a garden in which people express their worship through working in the tasks to which God instructed them. The Bible concludes with the new heavens and new earth being described as a city—a complex expression of organization and culture. This is how humanity ultimately expresses the dominion they were commanded to do in Genesis 1. They work, but their work is done for the glory of God, and is no longer frustrated by the Fall.

As a Christian, how should I think about my work?

For the Christian, work is an expression of worship. Work is neither the ultimate goal of human existence nor a necessary evil to sustain human existence. The ultimate goal of human existence is worship, and thus work is to glorify and honor God. Moreover, work is part of God's good, created order that remains good even though marred by the Fall. Quantifying a lifetime of work drives home the importance of viewing work as an expression of worship. If you graduate from college and work for the next forty years, you will spend over 80,000 hours at work. In contrast, if you invest six hours a week in church, attending and serving over those same years, you will spend more than 12,000 hours doing so. God desires us to view such a large portion of our lives as worship and glorifying to Him. In thinking about a Christian view of work a few questions are important: What should we do? How should we do it? And Why should we do it?

What? (content): We tend to focus our conversations about work on "What should we do?" Typical answers are "whatever makes you happy," "whatever you are passionate about," or "whatever enables you to retire the soonest." The Bible does not spend much time talking about what kind of work we ought to do. Perhaps this absence is due to people in those times rarely having much opportunity to choose what they might do with their lives. Nevertheless, the question of "what should I do?" is still important. Christians should not engage in immoral activity as a form of work. The Christian must not violate God's moral commandments as a way to fulfill the mandate to work. For example, the Christian must not "work" in a way that steals from others. While immoral work might accomplish good things like providing for one's family, it is still unchristian because the nature of the activity is unchristian.

How (manner): Perhaps because most of the people in the Bible had little choice in their occupations, and thus might have done things they would not have preferred to do, the Bible says a lot about how we should work. To people working in a far from ideal situation, Paul instructs them to work "not by way of eye-service, as people-pleasers, but with sincerity of heart, fearing the Lord. Whatever you do, work heartily, as for the Lord and not for men, knowing that from the Lord you will receive the inheritance as your reward. You are serving the Lord Christ" (Col. 3:22–24). Christians must not only render "eye-service" in the sense that they work so long as they are being watched—that kind of work lacks integrity and does not acknowledge that God sees everything. We ought to work with sincerity—giving a good service—and heartily—to the best of our capacities. God is concerned not just with what we do but with how we do it.

Why? (motivation): Good work that is done in the right way with the right motives—no matter how menial or personally unfulfilling—is "serving the Lord Christ" (Col. 3:24). Christians must view their work as a way ultimately of serving God. The Bible reminds us that "whatever you do, do all to the glory of God" (1 Cor. 10:31). So the motivation for all Christian work is that it is done for the glory of God in the service of Christ. With this primary motivation of work, there are several secondary motivations. Christians with families ought to work to provide for the family God entrusted to them. The person who is unwilling to work to provide is truly non-Christian (1 Tim. 5:8). Through diligence, the Christian might also "have something to share with anyone in need" (Eph. 4:28). Indeed, Christian care for the poor and vulnerable is founded on the presupposition of diligence to provide for needs (see Rom. 12:13; Gal. 2:10; Heb. 13:16). Finally, Christian work should be a testimony to nonbelievers of the heart that is set on God (1 Thess. 4:10). Lazy Christian employees do not have a compelling testimony before their bosses and coworkers.

Conclusion:

Christians ought to work. And Christians ought to work in a manner that is God-honoring because their whole lives are dedicated to the worship of God. The danger with work is that Christians can move from faithful fruitfulness into idolatrous directions. They might idolize rest so that they fall into idleness. Or they might idolize productivity, so they fall into workaholism and an identity determined by their work. The Bible calls us to view work as an expression of worship— originally part of God's good design, presently a way to worship God even in the world's brokenness, and eternally restored to its effective and unhindered purpose.

Reflection Questions:

1. What ideas about work do I borrow from my culture? Do these ideas align with a biblical view?
2. What you do, how you do it, and why you do it are all important to God. What are godly motivations for work, even work that you might not like?
3. Which God-given responsibilities in your life are you tempted to prioritize over God Himself?
4. As you think about how work is portrayed in the broader cultural conversations, how does the Bible correct misunderstandings about work?

8

Wise Habits of Work

How can I be effective at work?

Have you ever sat around a campfire and recoiled at the sting of smoke blowing in your eyes? That experience has more to do with your work than you may realize. In college at a state university, I (Jon) served as a student leader in an outreach ministry to the campus. As upperclassmen, we would return to college early and help move in the first-year students on orientation day. Move-in day was wonderfully effective in building relationships with new college students, hopefully leading toward spiritual conversations and inviting people far from God to faith in Jesus. A training session for that move-in day left a powerful impression on me.

My mentor, a staff leader in the ministry, spent some time telling us how the everyday, ordinary work of carrying boxes into a residence hall was far more significant than it appeared at first glance. This service would open the door to relationships and, in due time, sharing the life-transforming message of Jesus Christ. He shared the significance of serving. He also helped us understand *how* we worked was more significant than we realized. If one of us on the team exhibited a lazy streak, it would hurt the overall impact of the ministry because it would discourage or frustrate others. If we did the essential work with a bad attitude instead of a cheerful heart, those we were serving would see right through the external effort, and the positive impact would be minimized. What about the campfire smoke? My mentor used the image to convey the effect of a poor work ethic. A wrong approach to work is like smoke in the eyes of the others on the team and those we are serving.

Carry this principle into the career you are preparing for as a college student. Not only does work matter because God designed it, but how we work matters. Our ultimate significance is not found in climbing a career ladder, but we are called to excellence in our work to represent Christ. A happy by-product of embracing wise disciplines of work is that Christ will be represented well, and it generally brings success because the world recognizes what God values, even if they don't know why. Let's consider some ways God intends us to work.

Habit 1: Work like you are working for Jesus, not just a human boss.

In many ways, this first habit of wise work is a mentality that unlocks the others. Colossians 3:22–25 provides a job description of working everyday jobs for the Lord. The world of the New Testament includes a facet of work many in the West are generally not accustomed to these days. A significant portion of the population worked within an economy of compelled labor. Employment for some was not voluntary under a system of slavery. In such circumstances, the New Testament provided a bold vantage point. Work for another was more than just something to be done as a minimum to satisfy expectations of a human overseer. Colossians 3:22–23 states, "Bondservants, obey in everything those who are your earthly masters, not by way of eye-service, as people-pleasers, but with sincerity of heart, fearing the Lord."

Many readers of this book will be able to choose their employer and many preferences about their career trajectory. This was not the case for most of those to whom Paul was writing under the rule of the Roman Empire. Similarly, many Christians around the world today do not have the same freedoms we have in the West to choose employment

Wise Habits of Work

arrangements. We must acknowledge the historical reality of Paul's instruction and recognize that His words are significant for us even when our circumstances are voluntary.

There is a higher relationship in play. The servant is called upon to serve sincerely, fearing the Lord. In any morally acceptable job, we can conceive of our work as being for God. God knows your station in life and the work you are doing. In God's governance of all things, we do not see how a particular task may fit into a much larger picture of His way in the world. While strange to our modern sensibilities, the notion of everyday work being for the Lord tracks back to creation. The first people, dwelling in perfect harmony with their creator, were commissioned to work toward the fruitfulness and dominion of creation as a reflection of their creator. Even in far less glamorous circumstances, this aspect of work remains.

Let's consider an example of a delivery driver. From one vantage point, the driver's job is to deliver a package for the online retailer. This could be done under the perspective of merely satisfying a boss's expectation for a quota of deliveries. That quota feeds into a corporate bottom line and the stock prices of shareholders. All this is mundane and common in a sense.

On the other hand, that delivery can be done as worship as part of God's bigger purposes. That job is how God has answered the prayer: "Give us this day our daily bread." Work provides for our means and those who depend on us. Our daily bread does not mysteriously fall from the sky but is purchased with our wages at a grocery store, where it was delivered by a driver who picked it up from a bakery that received ingredients from a farmer. The Apostle Paul reiterates this point when he states that if one "is not willing to work, let him not eat" (2 Thess. 3:10). Such a person misses the reality that working for the Lord is God's general design for meeting human needs.

On another horizon, the Lord sustains and governs more than we realize through work. At least in some cases, it may happen that the package you delivered will contain an item essential in the chain of God's work. A book that will shape a person's ideas and change their future. A device they will use to communicate with others or to create content that impacts lives. Ordinary supplies to sustain their home living environment to be used for hospitality and blessing others. Extend that thinking to whatever work you will do in your career after graduation. Computer science, programming, and cybersecurity. Engineering. Education at all levels. Social work. Healthcare. The list could go on. The routine tasks of those jobs can and should be done for the Lord because He is at work in unseen ways through what appears to be unspiritual.

The practical effect is a mentality shift that views work as for God and as a means of worship. This mentality comes with an assurance in Colossians 3:24–25. God sees and knows. You are serving Christ even though you might work for an employer who is nothing like Jesus. How? God is at work through your work to meet your needs and the needs of others. He sees and knows you in your work. Ultimately, God will reward faithfulness, even if it does not come in earthly promotions.

Habit 2: Demonstrate godly character

Words like integrity, excellence, trustworthiness, consistency, respect, and ethics are all words that arise in corporate settings to describe the attributes of valued employees. Flip over to Chapter 5 on character, and you'll see those ideas are not the invention of the marketplace. There's something universal about how God designed humanity to flourish. Godly characteristics are also the attributes that generally lead to a positive impact in organizations. This reality about life should be no surprise for Christians. The good news is Christians who take character seriously are often positioned to succeed at work.

While character is generally valued and can position Christians for success, character does not always produce an ideal outcome. Times will arise throughout your career when it will be challenging to maintain your integrity. A supervisor may expect you to lie. The expectation and pressure may come through misrepresenting facts to a client or outright stating untruths in a report to executives. In other settings, there may be an expectation to compromise by affirming what the Scriptures do not permit. Christians in the marketplace are sometimes expected to affirm moral issues related to abortion, gender, and sexuality. There are nuances to responding in each scenario that should involve seeking counsel in your church. Compassionately, gently, firmly, and boldly living with conviction of character is a noble calling. Prioritize choosing God's way every time; you will influence others around you and accomplish significant work.

Habit 3: Practice servant leadership

Anyone with a job, even with the best boss, knows that things can continuously be improved. The best employees understand the mission and take the initiative to influence improvement while rightly submitting to authority. The manager-employee relationship is the inevitable outworking of God's mandate to humanity at creation to exercise dominion. Even without a Fall, the trajectory of fruitful multiplication would seemingly have been societies, cities, and human beings relating to one another to fulfill the mandate. In modern terms, that relationship is in the context of companies, non-profit organizations, and institutions that employ people. The relationship is between employer and employee.

What does this have to do with how you work? Your job will be within an organization that has a particular mission. Your voluntary employment in that place affirms that you will contribute to accomplishing that mission. Inevitably, each organization makes practical decisions about how to achieve that mission. This produces a set of stated company policies and often unstated cultural practices. The wise habit of work is to recognize the mission and how those who cultivate the environment accomplish that mission. Then, serve that mission with simple integrity.

Does this mean each employee is a mere automaton? In healthy organizations, certainly not! Submission to the mission and way of accomplishing that mission is essential. The best employees are those who identify ways of improvement in their sphere of responsibility and implement it. Initiative is the habit that drives progress. Initiative will inevitably spill outside your immediate sphere of responsibility, in which case an artful appeal to those in authority can prompt change. Christians strive for excellence at work because that is one way of worshipping God. Strive to go above and beyond the basic expectation for a job because doing so represents Jesus well and serves others well. Wise work will respect authority and take the initiative to work for change for the benefit of others.

The ultimate expression of the balance described above is servant leadership. Servant leadership is characterized by striving to set an example, earning trust, meeting practical needs, prioritizing others, and distributing credit rather than hoarding credit. Viewing leadership through the lens of influence rather than position means you might become an influential servant leader even without a formal leadership position.

Habit 4: Find the balance between idolatry and laziness.

Humanity is a story of taking good things and turning them bad. Often, walking in holiness is recognizing when we are using something good in the wrong way. Work is no exception. Work is a good creation of God that tends to be met with one of two distortions. On the one hand, work can become an outlet for idolatry, such as building a name for yourself, placing an identity in achievement, living up to your parents' expectations, or financial greed. In this case, work becomes a master that places you on the treadmill of more and more until the cycle costs more than could be imagined. On the other hand, work can become merely a necessary burden in this world. Such a mindset produces laziness, manifesting lackluster effort or even cutting corners.

Those who "live to work" and those who "work to live" fall into the ditch on either side of the road. Each person tends toward one or the other of these errors concerning work. The first step toward wisdom is to recognize the tendency in your heart. Then, communicate about that with a trusted mentor as you seek to walk in wisdom. Along the way, the antidote is firmly rooting your identity in Christ rather than work.

Conclusion

Of course, many other habits related to work are worth mentioning. Treat people well. Be on time and reliable. Show initiative and be a problem solver. Develop your skills. The list could continue. To sum it all up, wise habits of work are unified by the pursuit of excellence in all you do. The pursuit of excellence results from the fact that all work is ultimately for Jesus Christ. Where worldly workplaces do not value work, there's a higher ambition for the work of any Christian. 1 Corinthians 10:31 establishes a comprehensive domain for how human activity can be done in the worship of God: 'So, whether you eat or drink, or whatever you do, do all to the glory of God.'

An appropriate way to land this chapter is with Daniel's example. Daniel stands as a shining example of wisdom and bravery. Yet, what enabled Daniel to demonstrate the greatness of His God in a lion's den? Work. Daniel worked with excellence (clearly with God's favor) to influence those around him. 'Then this Daniel became distinguished above all the other high officials and satraps, because an excellent spirit was in him. And the king planned to set him over the whole kingdom' (Dan. 6:3). You will not be conscripted to serve in Babylon's courts, but you will invest a significant portion of your life in workplaces. Wise work habits will glorify God and enable you to impact others. Start practicing now.

Reflection Questions

1. What difference does it make for your current work or career pursuits to have a mentality that you are working for Christ?
2. Do you tend toward idolatry or laziness in work?
3. How does the pursuit of excellence now express worship of God? How does it relate to your future career?
4. What wise work habits can you implement in your current job?

9

Choosing a Major

How do I decide what I should do?

There's much anxiety in approaching a fork in the road you do not understand. Where will one path lead versus another? What will I miss out on by going down this one and not that one? Will I be capable of completing the path I choose? Will I wish I made a different decision after it's too late to turn back?

I (Jon) remember the overwhelming feeling of preparing for college and the significance of thinking about what I would do with my life. Now, I'm grownup, and thankfully, so far, it has worked out beautifully. However, I must admit that the journey worked out differently than I could have predicted. For example, my undergraduate degree is a liberal arts-based pre-law degree. Rather than enrolling in law school after college, I earned master's and doctoral degrees in theology. On top of that, my intentions of serving in full-time local church pastoral ministry were redirected by the Lord into serving as an administrator and professor in higher education while seeking to serve the church as a lay elder. I'm confident I am right where the Lord wants me, and I'm also convinced each unexpected turn was by His design. I'm also confident nothing was a waste even though the pathway was not linear. However, I did not always have the confidence I possess now after seeing how it worked out. The anxiety-generating decision of my youth is often framed for students in the question, "What are you going to choose as your major?"

At seventeen or eighteen, this decision feels like taking a fork in the road that will lead to one reality and keep you forever wondering what was down the unchosen path. Add to the internal pressures you may feel the many messages that social media, family, friends, and perhaps even colleges add to this decision. The good news is the decision of what degree to pursue in college does not have to be this way. We cannot tell you what to major in, but we can give you a road map. In following this road map, we hope you will find selecting a major to no longer be a choice characterized by fear but rather a decision filled with peace and excitement about loving God and your neighbor through your future vocation. While the decision might be overwhelming, pause to express gratitude that you have some ability to choose your vocational direction. Many people worldwide today do not have the same freedom we enjoy in our economic and educational systems. Let's explore some things you should consider when choosing a college major.

Submit the entire process to God

Trusting the one who holds your future is the most crucial aspect of faithfully walking into the unknown. The character of God provides the entire atmosphere within which you can think well about your life and make wise decisions. God is all-knowing, so He is never surprised. God is all-wise, so He always does the best thing with the knowledge He has. God is good, so He always acts for your good. God is holy and righteous, so He will never lead you astray. God is all-powerful, so He can guide your life and protect you from harm. God is infinite and transcendent, so He rises above our limitations in decision-making. God is immanent (a theological word for near), so He draws near in love and grace to you in times of need. There's much more to say about the character of God, but this brief reminder ought to assure you it's always a good thing to submit to God a decision like choosing a major. Many people are on autopilot in making career decisions based on the type of lifestyle it will provide. In the United

Choosing a Major

States, this approach has been labeled "The American Dream." While success is a wonderful thing when achieved correctly, a shortsighted approach to selecting a major often cuts the Lord out of the picture.

The priority of life is to seek the kingdom of God according to His priorities. By seeking the Kingdom of God, we mean recognizing the Lordship of Jesus Christ over our lives and deferring to the priorities He sets for our lives in the Bible. Submitting your life to God is maintaining a heart posture that chooses His ways over lesser substitutes. While submission is an attitude of the heart to choose God's way over any other rival, some habits cultivate this heart posture.

The process of submitting to God starts with reading the Bible. God will not tell you what to choose as a major in the Bible. There's no chapter and verse for that. What God will tell you is the purpose for which you exist. He will tell you who He is and what He is doing with the world He created. He will tell you who you are and about your most significant needs. These truths are the realities guiding everything else about life and providing the orienting beacons for wise decisions. Without knowing what God has said about these topics, most people will inevitably supply their version. The wrong-orienting beacons often result in the wrong heading. Walk with the Lord, and He will walk with you through the decision-making process.

The second habit is prayer. Like Bible reading, prayer will not result in an instantaneous and scientifically proven decision. Approaching prayer that way is misguided. Prayer is communion with God in which we share our deepest thoughts and longings. We express our dependence on Him. Prayer demonstrates that we need God and are not adequate in ourselves. When deciding on a major, this habit of fellowship with God and depending on Him will put your heart in a place for Him to guide you. Without prayer as an expression of reliance on God, most people will lean into self-sufficiency and decision-making that functionally excludes God.

We like to feel like our circumstances are under control. When the unknown looms in front of us, we often grasp for control. Ironically, these attempts at control add little clarity moving forward. This is what happens when fear takes over from faith. The most important thing about your faith is not the strength you muster up. The most important thing about your faith is the God in whom you place your faith, as even weak faith in our strong God is transformational to life. Walk daily with the Lord and trust He will guide you. Upgrade the following verse from intellectual knowledge to one you are living, and you will not lose.

> Trust in the LORD with all your heart, and do not lean on your own understanding. In all your ways acknowledge him, and he will make straight your paths (Prov. 3:5-6).

With your life submitted to God, you can follow the four steps below in choosing a major.

Step 1: Do not overcomplicate the process

While it is essential to submit the process to God as part of submitting your life to Him, we should also not over-spiritualize the decision. Many Christians think of God's will as always consisting of a precisely defined path. The idea is that God expects us to follow a specified series of steps with every life decision, and deviating from that path is disobedience. We assume Scripture presents God's will regarding life decisions as one singular path that is the key to unlocking blessing. The Bible does say a lot about God's will, but often not in a specified manner about your life decisions.

The Bible tells us that God's will is to put Him first and live by His priorities. God's will is for you to follow Jesus in faith and live well in the world. From there, in many cases, God is pleased for you to use your decision-making to choose one of a variety of options that could bring glory to Him. God's will on choosing a major is more like playing freely on a field. The field is defined by God's boundaries (His holiness), and the game is determined by His rules (life for His glory). While the

Lord may want to guide you to a specific major, most often, we find He does not express His will for our lives in that way. God often grants those who put Him first the freedom to discern and choose pathways within their circumstances in life. Your desires, skills, experiences, family background, and academic ability are common influences the Lord uses to shape where and how we will work.

One way we tend to over-spiritualize our work is to make decisions solely based on our "passions." This advice cuts against the standard narrative of colleges and contemporary career advice. We are often told to pursue our passion and intertwine our work and our passions. The world also preaches that there are no limits and you can be anything you want. A desire for what you will do with most of your waking hours is not wrong. There are ways in which it is healthy to find some measure of enjoyment in our work. It is also the case that life is full of limits. The prevailing mentality has shifted out of balance toward only going to work if it is a "passion." A career is about serving God and others through the ordinary means of job responsibilities.

The real question is not "What has God given me a passion to do?" but "How can I use my resources to glorify God and serve others in a field that I am capable of and will generally enjoy?" This question is a healthier starting point because passions change, circumstances change, and it is impossible for any career ever to supply ultimate satisfaction. Put the focus on identifying what abilities, interests, and experiences you can match to a vocation and pick a major that enables you to step toward that vocation.

Step 2: Gain an accurate assessment of yourself

Different degree programs require vastly different abilities of their students. Some emphasize skills in creativity, composition, language, and the arts. Others lean heavily into science, technology, and math. Some will require high emotional intelligence for teaching children or exercising compassion in meeting relational human needs. Others will require the ability to bear with the physical health of people, which inherently involves tolerance of illness, blood, and bodily fluids (there's a reason I'm not a doctor). What can you do, and what are you not built to do? Answer this question for yourself, but also recognize sometimes we need other people to help assess. Things you think are your weaknesses might be a lack of confidence or experience. Things you think are your strengths might be a matter of prideful blind spots. Ask the people who know you to be candid about their perceptions of your academic and future vocational strengths and weaknesses.

Compare the strengths and weaknesses this process reveals to the kind of work required for a degree program. Don't stop there. A degree is a temporary experience, but the daily work of a career might require different loads on your strengths and weaknesses than the degree to get there. Most importantly, compare your strengths and weaknesses to what is regularly needed to work in the vocations you are considering.

Step 3: Gain counsel and experience

So far, you have identified the careers in which you are interested in utilizing your time and energy to glorify God and make a difference in the world. You have also identified the abilities and desires that shape the careers it would be possible for you to pursue. List viable careers and jobs you have heard of after those first two considerations. The next step is to seek experiences and counsel that can inform your decision-making. There are a variety of ways to pursue this next step.

- Informational Interviews – Identify people you know who work in the career fields on your list. There are likely people in your church who work in these fields and would be delighted to help you. Share with them that you are interested in their career field as you consider selecting a major for college. Ask them to meet with you for an hour and ask them questions about their job, how

Choosing a Major

they got into it, the positives and negatives, and their advice about going into their career field.

- Shadowing, Internships, or Volunteering – Once you have conducted a round of interviews for each career field on your list, look for an opportunity to experience the career firsthand. These experiences range from shadowing someone for a day to a summer internship. Start with the network you've already formed in the informational interviews and explore opportunities in the daily business of a career field. This experience will significantly clarify how the work intersects with your desires and abilities.
- Seek the Counsel of Godly Professionals – When people are unavailable within careers on your list, you can access the counsel of godly professionals from another field. Many experiences translate across career fields, and most advanced people have worked in three to four different career fields on their way to their current job. Listening to the experience of a godly person working excellently in their career will provide a basis for thinking about any career. Identify a person or two and ask them to share their career experience and advice.

The experiences above will equip you to make informed decisions. The more you explore the possibilities, the more information you have to support your decision-making.

Step 4: Decide and get started

The first three steps bring you to the day you need to declare a major for college. Take all you have gained through this process, spend time with the Lord in the Word and prayer, and decide! Another way to summarize the points above is to pick a degree that meets the following four criteria.

- Does the world benefit from it?
- Am I capable of it?
- Do I desire to do it?

- Will I financially provide for myself and Kingdom ministry through it?

The sweet spot is where these four facets of a career overlap. It certainly is not realistic for every task of every job to perfectly fulfill all four criteria. However, when you can generally affirm each of these aspects for your work life, your efforts align with God's design for vocation.

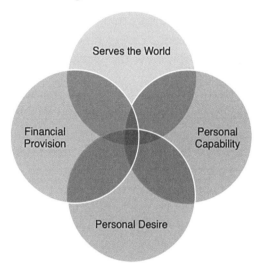

A wide range of vocational pursuits glorify God when they meet these criteria and are done in worship. What if you are still not entirely sure in only one direction? That is ok. You should not expect to have 100% certainty about your chosen direction. It's even possible for your answers to these criteria to change over time. You need to choose and be at peace with that decision, but it is reasonable to have only a degree of confidence in your decision. You will continue to learn and gain experiences that will either affirm your direction or nudge you in a different direction. Release yourself from the expectation that you must be confident in this decision as though there could be no possibility you will end up in a different major by the end of college. Expecting absolute certainty from the beginning is unrealistic for how the future might unfold. Own your decision confidently, but do not be paralyzed by a desire for certainty.

You might have inklings about what you could choose as a major, but you are far from convinced it's your definite pathway. The lower your confidence, the more you should select a degree with higher flexibility. In such a scenario, identify degree programs that allow the flexibility to register for credits early in college that will keep your option to change in your first year or two without losing progress. When choosing a major, it is better to get it right than fast.

Finally, remember an undergraduate degree is a foundation, not the entire determination of your life. Most students feel like they are deciding everything about their future at eighteen. This is not helpful pressure. While this feeling is understandable, it does not represent reality. Remember that various careers can be pursued from the foundation of any major. Many professionals will work in multiple vocational fields throughout their careers. Some may never work directly in the field of their undergraduate degree. Even so, the skills, knowledge, and maturity they gained through earning a degree are all a foundation for future endeavors.

Conclusion

Take a deep breath. Start by submitting your life to the Lord. The good news is that God wants to use your life for His glory and guide you to good things even more than you want those things for your life. Rest in the reality that He knows you, cares for you, and will provide for you. God will grant you direction as you practice the steps above to discern how to glorify Him and serve others through your education.

Reflection Questions

1. Are you submitting your entire life to the Lord and seeking to walk with Him regularly in Bible reading, prayer, and fellowship in your church?

2. Have you been thinking about God's will for practical decisions as a specified linear path to walk or a field on which to freely play and create under God's rules?
3. How would you summarize an accurate assessment of yourself regarding possible degree programs and careers?
4. What next step can you take to gain wise counsel and experience to inform your decision-making?

10

Great Commission Living
How do I leverage my whole life for the gospel?

You know it because you've seen it in dozens of places. On the church wall, in a mission agency brochure, or on a coffee mug in your cabinet at home. These are the words just about every Christian knows, but Christians rarely own. We're talking about the Great Commission—the direction from Jesus to make disciples of all nations. Even though the words from Matthew 28 are well-known, there is a lot of confusion about the Great Commission. Many Christians treat the Great Commission as the responsibility of those only in vocational ministry. Another distortion is that we can also think of the Great Commission as a few spiritual activities operating in the margins of everyday life. In contrast to the muddied waters, we hope to show you how the Great Commission is for every follower of Jesus and runs through all of life. God is building something magnificent through disciple-making, and every believer can be part of God's mission regardless of their day job.

What is a disciple?
Our authoritative guide for how to make disciples is the New Testament. It is noteworthy that the New Testament does not provide a conceptual definition of disciple-making. Instead, we are given a biographical definition through stories and

instruction. Starting with this biographical method of defining disciple-making, we can conclude that being a disciple is faithfully following Jesus in the general example of His first followers. This journey of following begins with initial faith in Jesus Christ. This faith includes ultimate commitment to the Lordship of Christ over all of life. And finally, the learning of a disciple is not only the cognitive content of truth about Jesus (though it is never less!), but it is also learning the way of transformed living with Jesus as master and teacher.

Biographically, we have an abundance of instruction regarding the "what" and "how" of making disciples. Given the model of Jesus and His disciples, our starting point for disciple-making is imitation. As one moves from the ministry of Jesus and His disciples through the growth of the New Testament, we see great consistency and further details emerge. To summarize, a disciple is:

- A Follower of Jesus (Matthew 4:18-22)
- A Student of Jesus (Matthew 10:24-25)
- A Confessor of Jesus (Matthew 16:13-20)
- A Sufferer for Jesus (Matthew 16:24-25)
- A Member of Jesus' Community (Matthew 18:15-20)
- An Ambassador for Jesus (Matthew 28:16-20)

A disciple is a person who has confessed Christ as Lord in faith, learns from Jesus, prioritizes following Jesus, invests in Jesus' community (the church), and seeks to fulfill Jesus' mission.

How do we Make Disciples?

Now that we have looked at the picture of a disciple, let's turn our attention to making disciples. The command to make disciples is simultaneously personal and corporate. Jesus' teaching and the examples of disciple-making in the New Testament make this clear.

The corporate side of disciple-making might surprise you, but it makes sense if we start at the beginning of the story to see the big picture. The mission of God has always been to dwell in life-giving fellowship with humanity. In the Garden of Eden (Gen. 1–2), Adam and Eve were created to live in union with God. The entrance of sin disrupted this relationship with God and introduced implications beyond our comprehension. Thankfully, in the face of this rebellion, God promised an eventual and ultimate conquering of the sin that separates humanity from God (Gen. 3:15). The victory over sin was accomplished in Christ, such that anyone who places their faith in Christ as Lord is transformed from death to life.

As amazing as this personal aspect of salvation is, what God is doing collectively is essential. Before the cross, God formed a nation to be His people. Through Jesus Christ and as a result of the cross, God has formed the church to be His people. God has formed and continues to create a people for Himself by multiplying disciples. The pattern is this:

1. The gospel is proclaimed (the Word of God).
2. Individuals repent of their sin and place their faith in Christ (Salvation).
3. Those new followers of Jesus are bound together to follow Jesus in a community (Church).
4. Those followers of Jesus cooperate to reach more people with the news of Christ (Great Commission).

Jesus made disciples, and the church was born. Individual disciples in churches make disciples through evangelism and life-on-life teaching, and more churches are born. This process is the Great Commission Jesus modeled for us and gave us to continue. Churches are filled with everyday, ordinary people. Those people work jobs, have hobbies, play at the park, and live in neighborhoods with the people Jesus Christ died to redeem. Those everyday, ordinary church members are best positioned to reach the people in their circles of work, neighborhood, and hobbies. In this way, the Great Commission is for every follower of Jesus because it is for every member of the church Jesus died to establish.

Moreover, the lost world will never be reached, and disciples will not multiply if ordinary church members are not filling their roles in the Great Commission every day. The normal, growing Christian will be a church member, and the typical result of a healthy church is the multiplication of disciples, which will result in the multiplication of churches. Then, new churches reach new people with the gospel, who grow into new disciples who start new churches. The entire process encapsulated in the words "Great Commission" is a divinely designed flywheel of momentum that can change the world one small relationship at a time.

God is doing something corporately, but how does living the Great Commission look on a personal level? The text of the Great Commission itself is instructive for us.

> And Jesus came and said to them, "All authority in heaven and on earth has been given to me. Go therefore and *make disciples of all nations, baptizing* them in the name of the Father and of the Son and of the Holy Spirit, *teaching* them to observe all that I have commanded you. And behold, I am with you always, to the end of the age" (Matt. 28:18-20).

The command is to "make disciples of all nations." We know from our earlier definition that a disciple is a confessor of faith and a follower of Jesus. We know from the Scriptures and the state of the world today that not all people are confessors and followers of Jesus. Therefore, the obvious first step in making disciples personally is to invite others to place their faith in Jesus and follow Him as Lord. We often call this first step of disciple-making "evangelism."

The next step in the Great Commission is "Baptizing them..." Jesus modeled baptism for His followers. Baptism is an enacted picture of Jesus' death, burial, and resurrection (Rom. 6), which is the pivotal work that accomplished any individual disciple's salvation. Baptism is the public identification of the disciple with the Triune God. Baptism is also the entrance into the church, and the life of corporately following Jesus described earlier in this chapter. Therefore, baptism in the Great Commission is a byword for teaching a new disciple to trust Christ entirely as Lord, fellowship with the Father regularly, and become part of Christ's body in the bond of the Holy Spirit. Baptism also indicates the normal arena for ongoing growth is the local church. Therefore, individual Christians do not randomly baptize people, but churches baptize disciples to acknowledge them as disciples, welcome them into the fellowship of disciples, and influence them toward ongoing Christlikeness.

Finally, the third step of the Great Commission is "teaching them to observe" all that Christ has commanded. You might be tempted to think this teaching step is where your pastor or some other ministry professional takes over. Those folks are essential indeed! But the teaching here is that every follower of Jesus teaches others how to follow Jesus. The earthly ministry of Jesus is the premier example of how we should accomplish the teaching required of us. Jesus taught the disciples through the Old Testament Scriptures, which He considered the Word of God. He also taught on His divine authority through His own words. In addition to imparting the Word of God, Jesus invested personally in the disciples by simply living with them. He used everyday moments of life to impact and model kingdom living. We follow Jesus' example to make disciples today by imparting the Scriptures and personally investing in people's lives. Paul expressed the same approach to personal disciple-making in 2 Timothy 2:2.

To summarize, the Great Commission is the activity followers of Jesus undertake to do the following:

1. Invite people far from God to experience salvation through faith in Christ expressed in repentance of sin and trusting Jesus as Lord.
2. Incorporate every new disciple of Jesus into the body of Christ as a meaningful member of a "local church." Personal disciple-making intersects with corporate disciple making, at the point individual evangelism and teaching lead to baptism and membership in a church.
3. Teach the Word of God and model faithful living in life-on-life relationships.

4. Invest in an existing disciple-making church and strive to establish new disciple-making churches to reach the lost.
5. Repeat and multiply steps 1–4 until the nations are reached!

Now that we have unpacked the Great Commission, what does this have to do with most things in life? Most of life is lived in your neighborhood, at work, in the grocery store, or on the internet. Many people think the Great Commission is going on a mission trip. We miss a massive opportunity for our lives to make an impact if we do not connect the Great Commission to everyday life. As a first step, all you need to do is look at your life right now. It is no accident that you have the friends and family you have. It is not happenstance that you live in the neighborhood you inhabit. It is not coincidental that you share hobbies with the people you hang out with or that you have specific coworkers at your workplace. Those people are in your path as those who need to hear the gospel of Jesus Christ and be discipled by you! Your church membership is directly related to these relationships as well. You gather as a disciple with other disciples in your church, only to scatter once again to live as bright lights in a dark world.

Conclusion

Rather than view some of life as spiritual and most as mundane, view it all as the field on which you can fulfill the Great Commission. In all the spaces and places of life, share the gospel message of Jesus Christ with people and invite them to follow Him in faith. Then, draw those who place their faith in Christ (new disciples!) into ever-deepening growth and fruit-bearing. You and your church can raise them to be disciple-makers themselves. Then, look at the world around you, determine a place lacking in gospel witness, and be part of establishing a new church there. The simple cycle of church life, being discipled, making disciples, evangelizing,

Great Commission Living

and starting new churches on repeat unlocks using all of life to fulfill the Great Commission.

Reflection Questions

1. In what ways are you currently involved in a church where you are discipled and you are discipling others? What steps should you take to further your involvement?
2. What younger or less mature Christians around you can you intentionally influence toward growth in Christ?
3. In your daily interactions, who are the people with whom you interact regularly who are not followers of Jesus? What would it look like for you to live out the Great Commission with them?

Part 3

Christian Apologetics

11

Truth

What is truth?

Connect to an internet network, and you will immediately receive many things that are not real. Your favorite social media feed inevitably includes fake news, filtered and modified images, and content produced by generative AI. Truth and reality are not only issues in everyday digital life but are uniquely a facet of intellectual life at college in most Western settings. I (Jon) was confronted regularly with this question while pursuing an undergraduate liberal arts and pre-law degree. In philosophy classes, the baseline presumption was that truth is not something to be discovered but a sentiment to be asserted. I remember this led a philosophical ethics professor to declare that even current criminal acts against children that any person with common sense would reject should be legalized. This radical conclusion stemmed from an underlying conviction that moral claims are not absolutes because there is no such thing as independent and objective truth. In literature and law, many claim that the meaning is not something an author communicates, and a reader discerns, but the reader supplies the meaning. From the halls of the ivory tower to everyday scrolling, does truth matter? While denying the truth might seem harmless in some situations, when carried to its conclusion, there are big consequences. That is why every college student must answer the question, "What is truth?"

Where do we start?

Since this is a book for Christian students about flourishing in college, we will begin at the source of truth – God Himself. Only God can define who He is and what is truth because He is God. We must listen to His witness about Himself to have any hope of understanding Him or the world He created. God is the center and originator of all reality (Gen. 1–2). His existence orients every other aspect of existence. God is truth and is, therefore, the model of truthfulness in that He perfectly manifests and communicates the reality of His nature. God is holy; therefore, He cannot lie or fail to keep a promise. Expressing untruthfulness would violate God's nature (Num. 23:19; Heb. 6:18). God's every Word is pure because God Himself is perfect in truth (Ps. 12:6). God's truthfulness means that He is the true God and that all His knowledge and words are both true and the final standard of truth. God's nature as truth and Jesus Christ as the perfect manifestation of truth in the flesh causes us to marvel. Jesus Christ claimed to be "the way, the truth, and the life" (John 14:6). Grace and truth came through Jesus Christ, and we know Him as the true God (John 1:17, 1 John 5:20).

God is truth, and God has revealed Himself in the Bible so we may know Him in truth. The communication of God through His word provides knowledge about God (2 Tim. 3:16–17). God is the initiator of all other reality through His act of creation. This means the ways God has designed creation determine reality outside of God. God's communication in the Bible about His creation, about things like the world and human nature, provides us with the truth about ourselves and the rest of creation (Ps. 119:160). Our judgments about what is true and not true are also measured by God as the center of reality (Zech. 8:16). Because He has revealed Himself in the Bible, we look toward God's Word to inform us about truth. In the Christian worldview, God has spoken and created reality. Human beings discover, know, and name reality. The biblical foundation that God is truth provides rich resources for how we think about all of life. However, dialoguing with postmodern professors and peers will likely not begin with quoting chapters and verses about God's nature. The good news is that the biblical view of truth is conversant with any worldview you encounter. Let's explore how to engage the question of truth with the world around you.

What is truth?

Truth is what corresponds to reality. Humans use words to make claims and communicate. When a claim corresponds to reality, that claim can be said to be true. When a claim does not correspond to reality, then that claim is not true. There are facts about the world – the sky is blue, water is composed of hydrogen and oxygen, God is love, and Abraham Lincoln delivered the Gettysburg Address. These are all aspects of reality that one could make claims about. If those claims correspond to the realities in play, then those claims bear the quality of truthfulness.

Jake might be color-blind, but that does not change the blue sky. Nancy might be superstitious and uneducated in chemistry, so she believes water is a mystical substance possessing the universe's life force, but that does not change the chemical composition of water as H2O. Frank might reject the notion of God's goodness because of personal suffering, but that does not change the spiritual reality. Edna might be a conspiracy theorist who claims history has been manipulated to control us today, but that does not change the sound waves people heard on the battlefield at Gettysburg from President Lincoln. In each exaggerated case above, the correspondence of the claims to the actual reality of the case determines whether one is truthful.

These examples are more than a philosophical game about perception, science, religion, and history. The realist approach to truth is significant because the correspondence of claims to reality is experienced in everyday life. A simple parable demonstrates the nature and significance of truth. Carson and Aaron are in the same premed biology class. Aaron missed the class session before their final exam because he was ill. The good news is he has a friend in the class who can relay the material and exam study tips provided by the professor. He asks Carson if the molecular genetics section will be in the exam's scope so he knows if he should study it. Carson informs him that the professor said the material will not be on the exam.

Exam day arrives, and the class works its way through the exam. True to Carson's word, molecular genetics is not on the exam. Remember that Aaron is sitting in a room with other students, experiencing the reality that they are not being tested on molecular genetics. It is the same reality for all. Yet, there is a facet of the experience for Aaron that his classmates are not experiencing. At that moment, Aaron experiences Carson's claim matching reality and is, therefore, true. Of course, there would have been significant academic and relational damage done to Aaron if Carson's claim did not correspond to reality. Truth is defined by the relationship between two things – a claim and reality. Truth is the quality attached to a claim that rightfully corresponds to reality. People experience flourishing when truth prevails and harm when truth is obscured.

What about the alternatives?

The alternatives to the correspondence-realist definition of truth are a variety of nonrealist views of truth. The common thread is that the correspondence to an independent reality does not define truth. Instead, truth is a human value attributed to a claim. What constitutes the legitimacy of this human value is what distinguishes the varieties of nonrealist views of truth. For example, the coherence view states that a claim can be true if it coheres with the other claims associated with it. In other words, if the claim is consistent with the entire system of thought one applies, it is true.

There are problems with this view of truth. The first is that the system of thought within which the claim exists is defined by the type of knowledge that is permissible. For example, one stream of historical thought claimed that only scientific

Truth

information obtained empirically is reliable knowledge. This limits any subsequent claims to a narrow definition of truth based on coherence. The problem only compounds when one realizes this claim about the nature of knowledge is not reached by scientific experimentation!

The second problem is that an entire system can be in error. Coherence alone does not make for truth; it only makes for consistency. It is possible to be coherently wrong or immoral. The coherence view has faded as a primarily philosophical influence because Western society has moved from Enlightenment-era thinking to its outworking in postmodernism.

More commonly, the nonrealist view of truth today is the pragmatic view. The pragmatic view states that a claim is true if it works. On the individual level, if it works for you, then it is true for you. In this case, truth comes from within and is self-authenticated by internal feelings and thoughts. Truth is not determined independent of an individual's perception based on whether it matches reality but is essentially granting ultimate authority to sentiments.

The pragmatic view of truth also operates collectively. Subcultures within societies conflict today because one group is asserting its version of truth. Furthermore, in this conflict, it is common for one group to claim that others' unwillingness to operate according to their version of truth is harmful and creates victimization. The missed step is searching for and acknowledging whether there is reality behind the claims of self-created truth. The postmodern view is that truth is an expression of sentiment or preference, a strong feeling about subjective reality, or a tool for power and manipulation.

The pragmatic view of truth brings to the surface the moral dimensions of how one answers the question, "What is truth?" In the realist view, truth is objective and external to the individual or group. It is accessible through knowledge. The outcomes of truth are beautiful and good. In the nonrealist view, truth is untethered and subject to the changing whims of individual or collective desires. The outcomes are inconsistent. It is worth noting the primary realms where people debate the definition of truth relate to morality, political power, and social position. There is no debate regarding the importance of a correspondence-realist approach to truth in realms like engineering, financial markets, and oncology. This dynamic reveals the actual concerns at play. There are several implications of the pragmatic, nonrealist view that disqualify it.

EQUATES TRUTH TO POWER: A weakness of the nonrealist view is that any claim to truth is viewed as an attempt to dictate power and control over another. This inherently includes acknowledging that the claim to this definition of truth is an attempt to assert power and control over others! The result is the pragmatic definition of truth is self-defeating. With the motivation of resisting power and control, the theory becomes a means of asserting what it seeks to eliminate—power and control. In other words, your truth is as good as my truth unless your truth gets in the way of my truth. At that point, the conflicting claim is no longer considered truth and can be eliminated.

INCONSISTENT APPLICATION: Not only is the pragmatic view self-defeating, but this view of truth is unlivable with any measure of consistency. Meaningful relationships are not formed when all statements are viewed through the lens of suspicion of power. Morality, virtue, and flourishing are not possible. Justice is undermined when there are no ways of determining truth from untruth. Living consistently with this view of truth is impossible, so morality must become selective. One must borrow from the realist view when it suits him and then resort to the pragmatic view when it aligns with his desires.

NO ARBITRATION: There is no means to arbitrate between right and wrong, truth and untruth, history and fiction, my way or your way. All that is left is the point above about equating truth to power. The question of truth becomes, "Who can assert their power over another?" This approach does not meet the ethic of love demanded by Jesus.

CLAIMS BECOME MEANINGLESS: Ultimately, claims become meaningless. Language is meaningful insofar as it communicates in ways that correspond to reality. When there is no quality of truth to claims in a fixed sense, language is cut loose to mean whatever one wants.

LOVE IS NOT POSSIBLE: Validating the desires and self-authenticated claims of others seems kind on the surface. After all, who knows what is right and good for them better than they do? Look past the surface, however, and it becomes evident quickly that there are more loving approaches than this. Love requires helping others see where their lives do not match reality, even when that is difficult.

Conclusion

Winston Churchill quipped about a political opponent, "Occasionally he stumbled over the truth, but hastily picked himself up and hurried on as if nothing had happened." Here, Churchill captures what is happening in contemporary society. While many people may claim truth is not universal, there is not a single human being who consistently denies in practice the existence of reality and the importance of people acting truthfully according to that reality. Fundamentally, very few people will embrace this view of truth in practice. For example, if you take your friend's sandwich out of his hands and start eating it, he would probably be upset with you. In that case, your truth (i.e., that sandwich belongs to me) is not valid to him. Press deep enough, and you'll find some point at which truth and falsehood matter to him. Every skeptic has inconsistencies in their worldview. When you seek to defend Christianity and share the gospel, ask good questions to help your friend see the incoherence of his worldview. If you are talking with a friend who embraces an unbiblical view of truth, press your friend to defend it. Provide examples of clear immorality in history and ask why those examples are objectively evil. Doing so, you will begin to poke holes in a view of truth that cannot withstand scrutiny. Then, you can provide a more compelling view of reality as described by our God in Scripture.

On your academic journey, not to mention in everyday relationships, you will undoubtedly encounter the claim that independent truth is an outdated and culturally constructed notion. Such claims inevitably reject reality and move to remake the world without a relationship with God at the center. Such a move brings significant consequences and does not function. Pursue truth, treasure truth, and flourish in the truth.

Reflection Questions

1. In your everyday, average way of thinking, do you seem to operate more so by a correspondence-realist or pragmatic nonrealist view of truth?
2. What are the implications of consistently operating by one view of truth over another?
3. C.S. Lewis said, "A man does not call a line crooked unless he has some idea of a straight line." What is the significance of this for truth?
4. Have you observed people arguing a point from different assumptions about truth? What was the impact of these unshared presuppositions?

12

Authority

Who defines what is right?

A tug-of-war over the issue of authority characterizes the modern Western world. In business, corporations wrestle back and forth for the ability to define the rules of commerce. In politics, candidates, political parties, and news channels debate at a fever pitch about who has the authority to determine the common good. In churches and religious organizations, leaders and members often struggle in a complicated dance of leadership and accountability characterized by conflict. Supervisors and employees frequently manifest strife as though one class of people must conflict with another for power. Sadly, with only a bit of personal thought – or reading a news feed – there are enough examples of misusing authority and power for some to conclude that authority is inherently problematic.

On a personal level, individuals wrestle with accepting or rejecting the authority of parents, educators, government officials, and even the general moral framework of the universe. Many times, the conclusion young adults reach because of the dynamics outlined above is that authority is inherently flawed. Of course, that is a convenient position until the young rise to positions of authority and find themselves seeking to figure out how to navigate the other side of the coin. While the roots of these authority struggles may be complex, Christianity offers a beacon of clarity. The Bible's wisdom on authority can guide us. God's Word provides peace and direction in a world often characterized by conflict and misuse of power.

The Authority over all authority

The biblical storyline includes the reality that anyone and everyone who ever holds authority is also under ultimate authority. The implication is that human authority is derived from God as ultimate authority rather than self-created. Authority is not equated with unfettered autonomy. On the contrary, authority is defined according to an external standard. The relationship of human authority to divine authority means it is bound in its very nature. The limits of any role of authority are demonstrated in contrast to the unlimited authority of God from whom all other authority derives. God's authority is established within Himself: no other declaration is needed outside of His nature to establish that He rightfully holds authority over all things. God is infinite in all of His attributes which include His power, truthfulness, righteousness, knowledge, and independence. All else depends upon God, who alone is entirely sufficient within Himself (Exod. 3:14–15; Acts 17:25). God's nature establishes that He possesses perfect authority over all else.

Jesus Christ is the perfect revelation of both divine authority and human submission. Jesus is truly God and truly human, the perfect union of two natures that manifests God's authoritative character and the perfect design for humanity. Jesus Christ is the one to whom all "authority in heaven and on earth has been given" (Matt. 28:18). Jesus demonstrated authority over creation through instances like healing the blind and calming the storm (Matt. 9:29; Mark 4:35–41). Jesus asserted the highest level of authority in His rightful power to forgive sin (Matt. 9:4–8). This claim of Jesus was controversial to His hearers because divine authority was demonstrated in humanity. Jesus' authority over all creation was established through His role in creating all that exists (John 1:3; Col. 1:16–17; Heb. 1:2–3).

Authority

Jesus is also the model of authority that rightly submits to authority as a matter of obedience. Christ's crucifixion was a moment in history where it appeared He was powerless in the face of worldly authorities and death. In a dialogue about authority, Jesus indicated to Pilate that His crucifixion was not a matter of lacking authority in comparison to Pilate, but that He willingly submitted to authority for a higher purpose (John 19:11). Jesus laid down His life, and through resurrection, demonstrated He was never displaced from ultimate authority. There was never a moment of powerlessness. There was only submission. The Son's submission to the Father, particularly in His earthly ministry, is a theme of the Bible that demonstrates God's rightful authority and the virtues of rightly ordering life under His highest authority. The authority of Jesus paired with His submission is shown throughout the book of John (4:34; 5:30; 6:38; 10:18; 12:49–50; 15:10).

There is practical significance to all human authority aligning under divine authority. There is objectivity to defining good and bad uses of authority. There is ultimate and final accountability for using authority, even when justice miscarries in human courts. There is a direction and purpose beyond individual or collective human desires to the use of authority. Christians are called to submit to various human authority relationships because God establishes them. Our hearts can rightly yield to authority even when we do not desire to because we recognize the relationship to a higher authority. Finally, there is clarity regarding when authority should not be obeyed because it contradicts God's higher authority.

Is authority good or bad?

There are two narratives regarding authority today. One narrative states authority is inherently wrong and to be viewed with skepticism. This view equates authority with power in such a way that power is always viewed to bring corruption. Lord Acton, a British historian of the late nineteenth and early twentieth centuries, famously stated that "Power tends to corrupt; absolute power tends to corrupt absolutely." This sentiment runs pervasively throughout the contemporary setting. It is not only the exercise of power that brings corruption to bear on people, but the status of any position of authority is problematic. History is filled with examples that give credence to Lord Acton's sentiment, such that many modern people have concluded power does not only *tend* to corrupt, it *necessarily* corrupts.

In this view, people who hold positions of authority are inherently rejected because all roles of authority are ultimately just the institutionalization of one person or group controlling another. This view of authority is rooted in evolutionary thinking that, when consistently applied, defines human relationships as winners and losers. Life is a game of power aimed at the survival of the fittest. Authority's source is that it is falsely created and gained over other people. We may still find examples of authority utilized for good, but the legitimate source is within the self. In a sense, in this approach, authority derives from autonomy. Authority can be directed toward the ends the individual determines, which makes it inherently dangerous and harmful (except, of course, for the person who happens to be in authority). Indeed, there ought to be caution about abuses of authority based on history alone, if not the sinful nature of humanity, as described in the Bible. Yet, does this mean authority is inherently flawed?

A contrary narrative is that authority possesses good roots and can accomplish good for the world when utilized appropriately. Authority is how parents protect and nurture children into healthy adults. Authority is how governments protect their citizens from evil. Authority is how the economic relationship of a society is organized in workplaces. It enables the everyday labor of people to create a world that meets the needs (not to mention the comforts) of those who inhabit it. Authority is an ingredient in how the church is built through congregations and pastors stewarding the authoritative Word of God.

Authority

This view of authority must ultimately be rooted in a view of the universe that there is an ultimate source of all of reality. The biblical framing of God as the source of all authority provides the best intellectual resource for the roots of human authority. The inevitable result of all existence being contingent on God the creator is that there is an ultimate authority. The Bible makes this aspect of God's existence abundantly clear in Genesis 1, Job, Romans 8, and Colossians 1. Infinite authority in the hands of God, who is perfectly good, resulted in the multiplication of life, fruitfulness, blessing, and peace. The setting of Eden pictures this reality perfectly. When Adam and Eve lived under God's perfect authority, they flourished and enjoyed a perfect relationship with Him. It was only when they sought to "be like God" and topple His authority that the effects of sin corrupted creation.

Echoes of the perfect result of perfect authority in creation come back in Isaiah 60, where the longed-for ideal peace is demonstrated in a natural world that includes counterintuitive images. Lions will graze on grass rather than hunt gazelle, children will be unharmed by what are now poisonous serpents, and predators will coexist with prey. All this idyllic peace is under the reign of a King who possesses all authority, has restored all things through His work of atonement, and is ruling forever in perfection (Col. 1:20).

Authority-generated peace demonstrates the contrast between perfect authority yielded by a perfect being in a world without sin and the world we know now. We inhabit the world infected by sin in a way that distorts the use of authority and its outcomes. The restoration of creation in a way that remedies the impact of sin demonstrates that the ultimate problem with authority is not its existence. Authority comes from a good source, is capable of healthy use, and can accomplish good ends. The problem is not authority; the problem is the sin that distorts the hearts of those in authority (and those under authority) to wield power selfishly rather than for others' flourishing.

What are the primary realms of authority in the Bible?

In the Bible, God establishes four primary realms of human authority. There is much to be said about the nature of each of these. The overview here is intended as only an introduction to the categories.

FAMILY

The first realm is the family. The Bible establishes early on that parents are in authority over their children, which means there are roles and responsibilities for each. Children are commanded to honor their parents (Exod. 20:12; Eph. 6:1–2). Parents are commanded to steward authority rightly over children through instruction, formation, love, and correction, which characterizes the virtue of healthy authority (Deut. 6: 5–9; Prov. 22:6; 29:15; Eph. 6:4).

CHURCH

The second realm of authority God established is the church. God did not design Christians to operate in isolation. The metaphors for the church in the New Testament are communal. They indicate the individual Christian is part of something bigger, whether parts of a larger body, citizens of a kingdom, or stones in a temple building. Christians are designed to be meaningfully connected to a church where they can be discipled and disciple others. The church also bears the responsibility for stewarding the truth of the gospel. Jesus brought these themes together when He stated His Lordship is the foundation for the church. Yet, to represent Christ in the world, the church would be responsible for advancing Jesus' rule and reign through His Word and relationship to the church (Matt. 16:13–19). The authority and nature of the church are explained in passages like Matthew 18:15–20, John 10:24–30, Titus 1:15, Hebrews 13:17, and 1 Peter 5:1–5. To be clear, the church does not control the salvation of any individual. Salvation is by grace through faith in the work of

Authority

Christ. Every individual is responsible for responding in faith to the gospel message of Jesus Christ. No church possesses the authority to dispense or withhold the grace of God. Only God holds that authority. The church, however, is God's designed organism for recognizing the salvation of individuals and discipling them into Christlike maturity. A local church is God's means for the authority of Christ as the head to manifest to the church's members as individuals.

GOVERNMENT

The third realm of authority established by God is government. Jesus demonstrated this nature of government when He instructed His disciples to pay tax to Caesar. According to Jesus, some aspects of authority rightfully belong to a government. Importantly, inherent in his acknowledgment of government is that the authority is limited. While a coin bears the image of Caesar and, therefore, that aspect of allegiance (paying taxes) belongs to Caesar, humanity bears the image of God (Luke 20:20–26). Therefore, only God holds the authority to be worthy of worship (Acts 5:29). Many Christians in our culture tend to have a negative view of governmental authority. Though there are likely legitimate concerns over any worldly government, this reflex does not match the teachings of the New Testament. Frequently, the apostles call the church to submit to government authorities, and these governments treated Christians far worse than our government treats Christians today. If Christians want to demonstrate in the public sphere the goodness of authority, one way we can do this is by submitting to and praying for government officials. The teaching of the New Testament fills out the picture of the government's authority as established by God in Romans 13; 1 Peter 2:13–17; and Titus 3:1.

WORK

The fourth realm of authority established by God is work. From the beginning of Scripture in the garden, humanity was commissioned to work in the created world. There is a nobility to work because it was designed by God, even though it is now marked by the curses of the fall. The inevitable outcome of a multiplying human population and ever-expanding advances in dominion was the relationship between human beings in work. In modern terms, the economic relationship inherent in the design is labeled in the workplace as "employee" and "supervisor." Like other authority relationships, the Bible instructs those on both sides. Those in authority are responsible for overseeing with fairness, justice, and wisdom because there is an authority over them (Lev. 19:13; Deut. 24:14; Luke 12:42; Eph. 6:9; Col. 4:1). Those who follow employers are to serve with respect, submission, and as though they are serving the Lord (Eph. 6:5–8; Col. 3:17, 22–25; 1 Pet. 2:18–21).

While God establishes the four realms above, they do not exhaust where authority is relevant to our lives. Some relationships are primarily entered voluntarily, which involves voluntary submission to authority. Enrolling in a school that requires a code of conduct is a willingness to abide under that authority. Joining an organization or ministry with institutional preferences to operate in a specific culture is a desire to maintain those practices under fair expectations. Even when authority can be welcomed and left behind voluntarily, it is a matter of integrity to abide accordingly while under the rule. Furthermore, God has designed authority to function for our good. When one rules rightly – whether a loving parent, a fair governor, a kind boss, or a pastor faithfully serving – those under their care flourish (2 Sam. 23:3–4).

Conclusion

We have shown that human authority is derived from the authority of God. Yet, for the good and flourishing of people, authority is God's wise design for order and provision. All human authority has limits because it is under God's authority. Similarly, all human authority is to be carried out with certain qualities. The essence of this for followers of Christ is evident in Matthew 20:25–28:

Authority

But Jesus called them to him and said, "You know that the rulers of the Gentiles lord it over them, and their great ones exercise authority over them. It shall not be so among you. But whoever would be great among you must be your servant, and whoever would be first among you must be your slave, even as the Son of Man came not to be served but to serve, and to give his life as a ransom for many."

Just as Jesus' authority was carried out through servanthood, so it is with His followers. Healthy authority is a servant expression of using resources, skills, and strength for the good of others. Healthy authority recognizes higher authorities in other entities and even teamwork. Healthy authority knows how to submit while also not becoming passive. Unhealthy authority is a domineering expression that seeks to make oneself great instead of being great. Unhealthy authority rejects higher authorities and strives for autonomy over teamwork. Unhealthy authority operates for the benefit of self rather than the good of others. The world is desperate for examples of healthy authority. Demonstrate Jesus to the world through rightly understanding and living according to His design for authority.

Reflection Questions

1. How does it influence your thoughts about authority that God is the ultimate source of human authority?
2. In what ways is God's design for authority different than how the world approaches authority?
3. What are examples you have seen of the healthy use of authority with the result that people under that authority flourished? What about negative examples?
4. What steps can you take now to live counterculturally according to God's design regarding authority?

13

Bible

Can I trust the Bible?

Certain kinds of documents incline us to either skepticism or trust. For example, we might read an autobiography with more scrutiny than a biography because we anticipate that an autobiographer will be inclined to present himself favorably. If you still read a newspaper, you might read an opinion piece with more critical thinking than a news piece that claims to present just the facts. And you might read a tabloid in the supermarket or information published by a political action group with even more skepticism.

Our skepticism or trust matters little for most pieces of literature. Whether or not I believe the news report about a political event in another country does not dramatically impact my life. But some things have massive consequences for my life. If, for example, I ignore a credible weather report about impending catastrophic storms, that negligence could severely impact my life. When we think about the Bible, it matters whether or not it is reliable and true. The Bible calls us to particular action—to believe that Jesus Christ is the Son of God who assumed human nature, died in our place for our sins, rose from the dead, ascended to heaven, and is seated as King. And the Bible declares that eternal life and eternal damnation depend on trusting in Jesus Christ. Some might claim that the Bible, if untrue, is inconsequential. But the Bible, if true, is of the utmost consequence. So, how do we determine if we can trust the Bible or not?

We acknowledge that this is not a comprehensive list of questions, and the answers are brief summaries rather than sustained arguments with extensive data. Space constraints, after all, are *constraining*. We intend this as an introduction to some of the issues involved in the discussion about the reliability of the Bible.

Why am I prone not to trust the Bible?

Not all questions about the reliability of Scripture are about the Bible itself. In fact, many of the challenges that people have with the Bible have more to do with their personal experience than anything else. Sometimes, a person has had a bad experience with Christians or a church, and this experience has led the person to reject the Bible and its message. Sometimes, the message of the Bible confronts someone's preconceived ideas about right and wrong, so the person concludes that the Bible must be untrustworthy. They have chosen to believe the truth claims derived from their inner intuition of right and wrong rather than the Bible. For example, I talked to someone who said, "The Bible endorses monogamy, and I am polyamorous, so I cannot believe the Bible." This person has looked at two truth claims and their sources (the Bible vs. the self), and the person concluded that the source of one truth claim was more reliable or desirable than the other. The challenge is that the "self" cannot support the weight of making decisions about ultimate truth claims. While we cannot address every personal issue that might cause someone to disbelieve the Bible, we can give encouragement to read and listen to the text.

Has the Bible come to us in a reliable way?

Many questions about the trustworthiness of the Bible center on the document itself and not the content of what is said. These are questions not about the claims that the Bible makes but about the reliability of the document's assembly, transmission, and translation. Volumes have been written about these topics, but we will summarize our conclusions briefly. Because we believe the Bible's claim to be inspired by God (2 Tim. 3:16) as the human writers were "carried along by the Holy Spirit" (2 Pet. 1:21), we believe that the Bible has the truthful and trustworthy character of God. Thus, we say that the Bible, in its original writing, is inerrant. The claim that the Bible is inerrant means it is entirely free from error (see chapter 2). But then, some people might question how the Bible gets to us.

ASSEMBLY OF THE BIBLE

One question focuses on the canon, the sixty-six books that comprise the single book of the Bible. Are the right books in the Bible? What about all the other ancient Judeo-Christian books that are not in the Bible? When we talk about the canon, it is essential to note that the church does not inspire or give authority to the biblical books; instead, the church receives and recognizes the inspirational authority that God has placed on the books and has made its mark on the church. From the beginning of the church, Christians recognized the authority of the Hebrew Bible, which we call the Old Testament. Between the last book of the Old Testament and the time of Jesus, there were some additional books written in Greek (the Apocrypha or Deutero-Canonical books) that Jews read but did not recognize as Scripture, and thus early Christians and contemporary Protestants also do not recognize them as Scripture.

The New Testament was written over several decades, and there is an awareness, even within the New Testament, that these books being written by the apostles were to be recognized as Scripture. For example, Peter says, "And count the patience of our Lord as salvation, just as our beloved brother Paul also wrote to you according to the wisdom given him, as he does in all his letters when he speaks in them of these matters. There are some things in them that are hard to understand, which the ignorant and unstable twist to their own destruction, as they do the other Scriptures" (2 Pet. 3:15–16). Peter associates the writings of Paul with "the other Scriptures." As the church recognized these authoritative books and collected them into a single canon, they used tests like *apostolicity* (that they originate with an apostle or close associate), *antiquity* (that they were old enough to have been apostolic), *wide distribution* (that Christians from multiple areas recognized and treated them as Scripture), and *orthodoxy* (that they are faithful to Christian doctrine, the rule of faith). Over the years, several additional documents with Christian-like elements have been proposed to be included in the canon, but they have always failed one of these tests.

TRANSMISSION OF THE BIBLE

If we affirm inspiration of the original documents and the proper collection into the canon, we still have to tackle the issue of transmission. Has the Bible been passed down in a trustworthy manner through the centuries? Many of these discussions about the reliability of transmission center on the New Testament. There are thousands of manuscripts of the New Testament, astoundingly more than any other ancient document. The earliest manuscripts were written in Greek, but early copies were made in other languages, such as Latin. With this many manuscripts, variants (i.e. differences between manuscripts) do exist among them. Most of these variant readings are either not viable (highly unlikely to be the original reading) or not meaningful (the various readings do not impact the meaning of the text). But there is a very small percentage of these variants (less than 1% by many scholars' calculations) that are viable and meaningful. The process of textual criticism is the study of these variant readings to discern what is the original reading. And there is broad consensus on the text of the vast majority of the New Testament. The reliability of the Old Testament is similarly strong. The earliest copies of the Old Testament were written in Hebrew. Similar to the New Testament, they were translated into other languages, and eventually, the Old Testament was translated into Greek. The use of the Old

Testament in both the early church and Jewish communities testifies to reliable transmission. The archaeological discovery of a large number of Old Testament copies known as the Dead Sea Scrolls affirmed reliable transmission. No other document is as widely (with the number of manuscripts) and reliably (with the agreement of words) attested as the Bible.

TRANSLATION OF THE BIBLE

Even with the questions of inspiration, canonization, and transmission settled, we still have the question about translation. Most of the readers of this book will read the Bible primarily in English, so we depend on English translations and, thus, translators. Are these translations faithful and accurate? The answer is that very many English translations are both faithful and accurate. Languages never map to one another in a one-to-one correspondence, so all translations involve some interpretation. But that does not mean that they are inaccurate. Translators operate with a translation theory or philosophy that articulates their priorities in the process of translation. We recommend translations that prioritize the original language more than trying to make an incredibly smooth English sentence. We also need to realize that while the Bible never changes, receptor languages (such as English) change regularly. What was a good English translation several hundred years ago might not be the best contemporary English translation. We also caution against translations that are the product of a singular individual. Almost all modern Bible translations are produced by groups of Christians who work together to render a translation that is accurate and clear in the language of ordinary readers.

What about the challenging claims that the Bible makes?

While many questions about the Bible's trustworthiness center on the Bible's textual history, a set of questions centers on the claims that the text of the Bible makes. The first set of questions (addressed above) asks, "Do we have the correct Bible?" This set of questions asks, "Is the Bible correct?" Again, multiple books have been written about each of these subcategories, so we can only make summary statements.

HISTORICAL FACTS

Some object that the Bible is not trustworthy because it inaccurately reports certain historical events. While not having space to address each of these specific claims, it is essential to understand how these claims are made. Typically, the Bible makes a claim that is at odds with some other historical document. When there is a fundamental disagreement between texts, one or both of them must be wrong. Often, these disputes are about details that are incidental to the main message (e.g., the existence or non-existence of an ancient city), but even incidental details are inspired, so we affirm them as true. In these cases, the skeptic privileges the claims made by other texts and thus concludes that the Bible is wrong. The real question is the presupposition of which of these texts is reliable. If you are in a conversation about the historical accuracy of Scripture with a skeptic, challenge that individual to identify specific instances in which the Bible has been proven to be historically inaccurate. More than likely, that person has received that claim as true without ever testing it. If someone is pushed to find a specific example of false claims in Scripture, they will be compelled to admit the events contained in Scripture have been confirmed by historians over and over again.

INTERNAL INCONSISTENCIES

So there are questions about when the Bible disagrees with other ancient documents, but what about the times that the Bible (allegedly) disagrees with itself? Sometimes, these are questions of numbers. We must acknowledge that there are different ways of reporting numbers. For example, how do you report the number of people who died in World War 2? Does that number include only those who died in battle, only soldiers who died in combat or other ways, civilian deaths from combat, civilian deaths from other factors of war, etc.? The point is there are often multiple accurate ways of reporting numbers, so we must account for the Bible reporting numbers in different ways. Another set of common accusations of internal inconsistencies concerns the parallel accounts of the gospels. It is alleged that when Matthew, Mark, Luke, and John tell the same stories, sometimes they tell a different story. Again, we must allow authors to emphasize different points while telling true stories. With any historical event, there could be multiple true accounts of the event. The differences are due to emphasis rather than factual inconsistencies. Christians have explained the issues of inconsistencies among the gospels for millennia.

UNBELIEVABLE CLAIMS

Then there is the objection that some claims the Bible makes are beyond reasonable belief. In the Old Testament, this objection involves something like the story of Jonah being swallowed by a fish or God sending a series of plagues. The challenge with these stories is that they deviate from our average natural experience. But that is the very thing these stories claim—that the God who created and sustains all things interacts with His creation in an abnormal or supernatural way. Similarly, when the New Testament reports that Jesus performs a miracle (such as healing diseases, feeding multitudes, or even raising the dead), the Bible claims that Jesus, Himself God in the flesh, interacts with creation in an abnormal or supernatural way. If Jesus is omnipotent God, then anything He does is within the realm of possibility. The question, then, becomes, "Is Jesus God?" If so, miracles are perhaps the most plausible thing we should imagine when finite humanity encounters an infinite God.

THE RESURRECTION OF JESUS CHRIST

This leads to the most unbelievable claim that the Bible makes—Jesus Christ is God in the flesh who rose from the dead. This most unbelievable claim is the central claim the Bible is calling us to believe. We can talk about the historical likelihood of this event by talking about the observable changes in world history. We can talk about the lives of the apostles who abandoned Jesus at the cross, yet nearly all died for Him after the resurrection. We can also talk about the reliability of the eyewitness accounts, and this is a claim that Paul himself makes in support of the truthfulness of the resurrection (1 Cor. 15:3–8). Ultimately, reliable eyewitnesses and historical probabilities will not convince someone to trust Jesus Christ as his or her personal Savior. That is, the message of the Bible must be received by faith. The prayer that we have for each person who reads this book is that God would shine "in our hearts to give the light of the knowledge of the glory of God in the face of Jesus Christ" (2 Cor. 4:6). Our prayer is that God would remove the blindness from hearts so that we might receive the message of the Bible by faith. Our prayer is that we would have not merely a historical confidence in the message of the Bible but a personal confidence in the message of the Bible so that we trust in Jesus Christ for salvation. Our prayer is that when we see "the face of Jesus Christ," we might respond in faith like Thomas, who was once a doubter but now believed and exclaimed, "My Lord and my God" (John 20:26).

Conclusion

The intended effect of reading the Bible extends beyond mere logical argumentation—God intends reading the Bible to shape your life and hopes in profound ways. And no amount of argumentation will convince someone that the Bible is the reliable Word of God. Logical argumentation shows that the verifiable facts of the Bible are true and that it has been transmitted to us remarkably well. But the message of the Bible must be received by faith. The greatest affirmation of the truthfulness of God's Word is to take it, read it, and see how God impresses it on your heart and life.

Reflection Questions

1. What are the most common doubts people express about the trustworthiness of the Bible?
2. How has your own experience of the Bible helped to affirm the trustworthiness of the Bible?
3. What is one of the most challenging questions you have about the Bible?

14

Humanity

What does it mean to be human?

Every generation has its central questions to be answered. Perhaps the most significant question facing students today is what it means to be human. From nearly every front, there are questions about what constitutes human life, the value of a human person, and a person's identity. In past generations, humans were understood to be unique in part because of their cognitive and critical reasoning abilities. Even more distinct is their ability to create art, poetry, and music. But modern artificial intelligence engines can seemingly think critically and compose artistically, and they can do it instantly. In past generations, humans were understood to be set apart from animals and thus had a unique status under the law. Still, recent lawsuits have argued that highly cognitive animals should have similar or equal status under the law. In past generations, human life was understood to have a certain dignity that should transcend commodification, but even the dignity of humanity is questioned today. These contrasts between former generations are nowhere more evident than with the issue of gender and sexuality. The claim, "My body is not aligned with my identity," seems to many people today to be the most "natural" of claims. But this claim would have made no sense to the vast majority of humans who have ever lived. To answer these central questions about humanity, we could look at any number of articulations throughout human history. However, as Christians, we believe that God has spoken truly and authoritatively through the Scriptures. He has told us who we are and what we are to do, and our first tasks are to listen, believe, and obey what He has said. Here is how the Bible describes what it means to be human.

How does the Bible describe what it means to be human?

BEARING THE IMAGE OF GOD

While the Bible first asserts that God exists and acts in the world, it is not long until the Bible explains the origin, essence, and purpose of humanity. The Bible describes the creation of humanity in Genesis 1 and 2. Genesis 1 describes God's creation of everything that exists and then describes humanity as the pinnacle of creation: "Then God said, 'Let us make man in our image, after our likeness. And let them have dominion over the fish of the sea and over the birds of the heavens and over the livestock and over all the earth and over every creeping thing that creeps on the earth.' So God created man in his own image, in the image of God he created him; male and female he created them" (Gen. 1:26–27). The issue of fundamental importance is that human beings are created in the image of God. While it might be challenging to describe the image of God in humanity, the image of God encompasses elements of both being and relation—who we are and what we are to do. The image of God is not reducible to any activity of humanity; instead, the image of God refers to the whole human being and the whole human race as a holistic declaration about how God has created human beings.

Every human bears God's image, meaning that humans resemble, represent, and relate to God in a way that is unique from the rest of creation. Humans resemble God, not just in cognition, sensation, and emotion. Even some animals have varying degrees of these capacities. Humans, like God, are spiritual beings (1 Thess. 5:23). An implication for this is that humans have a unique ability to relate to God, and God takes a unique interest in relating to humanity. One way that humans uniquely relate to God is that they are charged with representing him, particularly in their dominion over creation. Because humans have a unique status from the rest of creation as being created in the image of God, humans have a unique value. This unique value of humanity is restated when God reaffirms His commitment to humanity, "Whoever sheds the blood of man, by man shall his blood be shed, for God made man in his own image" (Gen. 9:6; see also Gen. 5:2). This reference in Genesis 9 is especially important because it affirms that the image of God is not destroyed by the Fall in Genesis 3. Human worth and dignity are not something humans must achieve; rather, human dignity is granted by the Creator, who forms each person in His image.

EMBODIED

The goodness of physical creation has been denied by many world religions and a few deviant Christian sects in history. But the biblical creation account repeatedly affirms the goodness of physical creation (Gen. 1:4, 10, 12, 18, 21, 25), with the concluding affirmation, "And God saw everything that he had made, and behold, it was very good" (1:31). The goodness of physical creation includes the goodness of the physical human body. Human beings are both immaterial and material in unity. That unity is separated only at death and awaits the reuniting at the resurrection (1 Cor. 15:42–49). We must affirm that God intentionally creates humans as both material and immaterial and, therefore, cares for both. The incarnation of Jesus Christ further attests to the value of the material aspect of humanity. Christians must affirm that Jesus Christ has come in the flesh (1 John 4:2), and thereby, Christians affirm the goodness of the material human body.

MALE AND FEMALE

God creates these human material bodies good, and He creates them in two distinct ways: "male and female He created them" (Gen. 1:27). It is crucial to notice that all human beings, both male and female are created in the image of God. There is no distinction among human beings with respect to their essence as image bearers.

Nevertheless, there is a distinction between men and women. This distinction becomes clearer when the creation account is retold in Genesis 2. First, "the LORD God formed the man of dust from the ground and breathed into his nostrils the breath of life" (2:7). Even with all the goodness of creation, "the LORD God said, 'It is not good that the man should be alone; I will make him a helper fit for him'" (2:18). God declares that he will create someone who is both like and unlike Adam. Eve will be like Adam in that she will bear the image of God, but she will also be different than Adam in that she will be female. And this complementarity of male and female is essential for them to fulfill their commission to "be fruitful and multiply and fill the earth" (Gen. 1:28).

These distinctions between men and women are part of God's good creation. For these first humans, and humans to this day, to fulfill God's calling for them, they must acknowledge their God-given maleness or femaleness and live in accordance with it.

FALLEN

In the biblical storyline, the untainted goodness of creation does not last long. Humanity rebels against God, and all creation is plunged into ruin. God had commanded them not to eat from a certain tree (Gen. 2:15–17). But they believed the lies of Satan more than the warnings of God, and they chose to eat from the tree. The consequences of their rebellion are devastating for their relationship with God. They are cast out of the Garden, and there is now a distance between them and God. The most devastating effect of the Fall is that they now experience the judgment of God for their sin (Rom. 5:12–21). They and their descendants now bear the curse of death so that they experience physical and spiritual death as they are "dead in [their] trespasses and sins" (Eph. 2:1). The effects of sin are not merely things that are recognized at the end of life.

Humanity

From this point onward, their bodies degrade and experience disease, their relationships are in turmoil (Gen. 3:16-19), and even their thinking is warped by this Fall into sin (Rom. 1:20-21). It is important to note that sinfulness is not an essential aspect of human nature. Humans existed without sin before Genesis 3, and those redeemed by Christ will exist without sin after Revelation 20. Moreover, Jesus Christ is fully human, yet He is without sin (2 Cor. 5:21). If sinfulness was a necessary part of human nature, then Christ could not have been both human and the perfect sacrifice for sin.

REDEEMABLE

By the total grace of God, these rebellious descendants of Adam are not hopelessly condemned in their sin forever. The Bible makes a comparison between all humanity being condemned through the rebellion of Adam and all humans who believe in Jesus being saved through the work of Jesus Christ: "For if, because of one man's trespass, death reigned through that one man, much more will those who receive the abundance of grace and the free gift of righteousness reign in life through the one man Jesus Christ" (Rom. 5:17). The impact of Adam's sin is experienced by all humans and the impact of Jesus' sinless sacrifice is experienced by all humans who trust in Him for salvation.

TRANSFORMED

If the physical body were merely something to be endured and discarded permanently at death, then it might be seen to be an evil of this world. But the biblical testimony is that Christ continues His embodiment and will transform our fallen embodiment to be glorious: "But our citizenship is in heaven, and from it we await a Savior, the Lord Jesus Christ, who will transform our lowly body to be like his glorious body, by the power that enables him even to subject all things to himself" (Phil. 3:20–21). These verses assume that Jesus Christ still has a glorious body. He ascended to heaven with His resurrected body, currently retains His full human nature (1 Tim. 2:5), and will return embodied (Acts 1:9–11). The assurance for Christians is that their physical bodies that are subject to death and decay in this fallen world will be transformed into an immortal body to dwell with God forever (1 Cor. 15:35–57).

What are the tensions between the biblical understanding of humanity and this cultural moment?

This biblical description of humanity presents God's created design as determinative for who a human person is and how he or she should operate in the world. We rightfully look back with horror on some of the ways previous generations denied this creation order. We are rightly horrified when we recount how previous generations denied the image of God in people because of their skin color, place of origin, ethnicity, appearance, cognitive ability, etc. We see that as a denial of the creation order in which God created every human being in His image. Awareness of historical failures creates an awareness that future generations might also recognize our current failures. And in our cultural moment, there is a common criticism of Christians as being on the "wrong side of history" when it comes to issues of human identity and sexuality. As Christians, our attempt must not be to locate ourselves in a position that future generations will judge as the right side of a historical trajectory toward progress. Rather, we must seek to live out and promote the view of humanity that God does—thus taking the longest view of history.

The current cultural crises are threefold. When does a human being become a person? When is human life no longer worth living? And who or what determines a human being's sexual identity and permissible sexual activity? We will leave the first two questions to other books, but our responses are not hard to deduce from what we have written above. The question of human sexuality is perhaps the most controversial in this current cultural moment, especially on college campuses. The fundamental question is, "Who has the authority to determine who I am?" Some historical answers to this question would include fate, society, family, etc. The radical claim of modern people is that nothing external to the individual can define that individual. It is the radical assertion that "I can be whatever I want to be at any given moment." Any attempt to constrain that identity is claimed to be repressive and a denial of personhood. Virtually everyone admits that I cannot be *anything* that I want to be or imagine myself to be. But there are certain realities about the self that our current culture is telling us that we can define: gender, sex, sexuality, etc. Tragically, our self-perception can be wrong. I might imagine myself to be physically fit, but that might be objectively untrue. So also, someone might imagine himself to be herself, but that too might be objectively untrue.

Just a few decades ago, people whose sexual preferences deviated from the norm would claim, "I was born this way" or even "God made me this way." These claims assumed there was order to the world, and they sometimes even attributed that order to God. But that rhetoric has largely changed. Now, the all-too-common yet radical claim is that "I can construct my identity however I want at any moment." And the expectation is that everyone else would affirm this person's self-determination without any question. The problem is that "self" can never bear the weight of defining "self." Human identity is not an individually determined reality at any given moment. As soon as human dignity is detached from the image of God, it becomes fragile and indefensible. As soon as human identity is detached from God's created order, it quickly expands into an amorphous, unsustainable idea.

Amid this cultural confusion, the Bible presents a clear and unchanging view of humanity that transcends culture and time. The Bible asserts that humans are unique among all creation because humans alone are created in the image of God. Thus, they have dignity and worth that is imbued by God Himself. The Bible asserts that human bodies are good, have a created design, and that God has purposes for how we use our bodies. Part of this good physical creation and human embodiment is the design for humans to be men and women. Biology, maleness, and femaleness are not accidental, but rather, they testify to God's created intention. They are normative created order. The Bible also asserts that the goodness of creation has been distorted and marred by the fall into sin. Sin permeates and affects all creation. This fall into sin is the genesis of the degradation of the body and confusion over its function. The reason that people might not "feel at home in their bodies" is a result of the confusion of sin. A person's confusion does not change the created reality. However, that person's experience of confusion and the cultural narrative to explain it make it harder to embrace God's created design and calling. When trying to understand ourselves—who we are and what we are to do—the question is whether or not we will believe what God has said in the Bible.

Conclusion

In former generations, it seemed "right" for groups in power to decide who was really human. But that decision was never entrusted to humanity. God has created all humans in His image, regardless of how humans attempted to define one another. In the current generation, it seems "right" to decide who I really am. But that decision was also never entrusted to humanity. God has created every human in His image, either male or female. And He expects us to affirm and live in accordance with His good, created order. While the current cultural counsel is to trust your feelings about who you are, we must trust God's counsel about who we are. God's design is excellent and deliberate, not ill-willed or accidental. God's design aligns with God's commands, and true freedom and joy are found by embracing both how God has designed us and how He has instructed us to live.

Reflection Questions

1. As you think historically, what are some differences between how human beings are viewed presently versus in previous ages?

Humanity

2. What are the most common cultural explanations of human identity and sexuality? Do they align with or contradict a biblical understanding of humanity?
3. In what ways might you not be living according to God's design of your human nature that you should submit to God?
4. What are your biggest questions about God's teaching on human nature, gender, and sexuality? Is there someone in your church with whom you could talk about these questions?

15

Exclusivity

Is Jesus the only way?

There is a reality about the world that troubles me deeply. Of the eight-plus billion people on the planet, more than three billion are "unreached." The unreached are people around the world who do not have access to the knowledge of the death, burial, and resurrection of Jesus Christ so that they may place their faith in Him and repent from their sins. These unreached exist within "people groups" who share a common culture and language. According to typical missiological data, there are approximately 17,000 people groups around the globe, with more than 7,000 unreached.[1] God's concern for the lost among the nations is set within a single context: His redemptive plan of salvation by faith in Jesus Christ. There are not many roads leading to eternal life, but only one way, one truth, and one life.

A question often raised in this discussion centers on the proverbial "Average Joe," living in a distant land and dying without hearing about the death, burial, and resurrection of Jesus Christ that makes salvation possible through faith in His name. What happens to Average Joe and, on a much larger scale, the three billion people who, if they died today, would never have had access to the gospel? This question is not just an intellectual exercise but a powerful motivation for evangelism. In what follows, we will see the answer Scripture

---

1.   https://www.joshuaproject.net

provides concerning the unreached and consider how this answer fuels the mission of Jesus' followers.

What does the Bible say?

The storyline of Scripture points to Jesus as the only way to salvation. From the early moments following the Fall, God makes a plan to save the people He created in His image. Eve, who rebelled against God's command, would one day, through her offspring, bear a child who would crush the head of the serpent and whose heel would be bruised in the process (Gen. 3:15). This promise of a serpent-crushing Messiah signaled the first indication of the power of God for salvation that would be fulfilled in Jesus Christ.

Throughout the Bible, an array of verses demonstrates that the early promise in Genesis of salvation through a Messiah was fulfilled exclusively in Jesus Christ. For instance, the idols and gods of the nations failed to provide a way of salvation compared to the spiritual power and deliverance found in the God of Israel (Pss. 96:5; 97:7). Jesus' claim for Himself is that He alone is the means to salvation: "I am the way, and the truth, and the life. No one comes to the Father except through me" (John 14:6). In his bold sermon delivered before the council in Jerusalem, Peter claimed that "There is salvation in no one else, for there is no other name under heaven given among men by which we must be saved" (Acts 4:12). Finally, the Apostle Paul made clear that Jesus Christ is the exclusive fulfillment of the law, making salvation available in Him alone (Rom. 10:1–4).

Some argue that those who are well-intentioned and seeking God will be saved based on humanity's universal access to God's general revelation in nature. This notion misses the biblical picture that sinful hearts inevitably suppress general revelation (Rom. 1:18–23). For example, in the one New Testament text where an individual responded to limited revelation, God did not regard that response as sufficient for salvation but supplied further specific revelation of salvation in Jesus Christ alone (see the story of Cornelius in Acts 10–11).

Exclusivity

The teaching of the Bible, though sometimes hard for people to accept, is that "no one seeks for God" (Rom. 3:9–12). Apart from the Holy Spirit's ministry of conviction and illumination through the Word of God, we do not seek God (1 Thess. 1:4–5; 1 Cor. 2:1–5). The image of the unregenerate heart is not one of a well-intentioned wanderer seeking truth but of an idol factory producing false worship.

As the commitment to the exclusivity of salvation through faith in Jesus Christ goes, so goes the missionary impulse of the people of God. The New Testament's motivation for evangelism is for the glory of God and the spiritual need of the lost. The command to go and preach the gospel flows naturally from the requirement of conscious faith in Jesus for salvation. On the other side of the equation, the assertions of universalism and inclusivism undermine the command to go and preach the gospel to the ends of the earth (Matt. 28:18–20). Universalism and inclusivism both assert that some, if not all, will be saved apart from faith in Jesus Christ. The God of Christianity is not the same as the gods of Islam, Buddhism, Hinduism, Mormonism, secularism, or any other belief system that denies the divinity of Jesus Christ, and this distinction carries an immense implication for humanity. As theologian Carl F. H. Henry was noted for saying regularly, "The gospel is only good news if it gets there in time."[2] Those who perish without placing their faith in Christ face the sobering reality of the judgment of God in hell.

The Apostle Paul makes this quite clear in Romans 10:14–15. First, faith in Christ comes only when the good news of Jesus Christ is understood and is met with the response of personal belief. Second, the unreached cannot believe in Jesus Christ if they have not heard of Him. Third, the only way the unreached can hear the gospel's good news is if someone proclaims it to them. Fourth, if they are not sent, the proclaimers of the gospel will not reach those who have not heard. This golden chain of God's design for saving sinners from among the nations is

---

2. Gregory Thornbury, *Recovering Classic Evangelicalism: Applying the Wisdom and Vision of Carl F.H. Henry* (Wheaton: Crossway, 2013), 175.

why taking the gospel to the unreached should be a concern of every Christian, whether it be sending or going.

Theologian J. Gresham Machen captured the impulse resulting from the exclusive nature of salvation:

> In answer to the objection [that exclusivism is too narrow], it may be said simply that the Christian way of salvation is narrow only so long as the Church chooses to let it remain narrow. The name of Jesus is discovered to be strangely adapted to men of every race and of every kind of previous education. And the Church has ample means, with promise of God's Spirit, to bring the name of Jesus to all. If, therefore, this way of salvation is not offered to all, it is not the fault of the way of salvation itself, but the fault of those who fail to use the means that God has placed in their hands.[3]

What about the objections?

The spiritual state of the world brings us to the uncomfortable truth that sometimes tempts us toward rationalizations and objections. There are five common categories of objections to the exclusivity of Christ. While the truth of the exclusivity of Christ is rarely popular, God's Word is clear and authoritative. Rather than dismiss the exclusivity of Christ, we should embrace it as an aspect of the glory reserved for the Son of God, and it should motivate us to evangelism. Consider the following objections to the exclusivity of Christ and responses.

THE FAIRNESS OBJECTION

Objection: "It is not fair that those who have never heard of Jesus Christ will not be saved. It is not their fault that they will never have the opportunity to hear about Jesus because of where they were born."

Response: Fair according to whose standard of justice? From the limited perspective of a fallen idea of justice, it might appear unfair, but it appears differently when considering the issue from God's perspective. No human being, other than

---

3.   J. Gresham Machen, *Christianity and Liberalism* (Grand Rapids: Eerdmans, 2009), 105.

Exclusivity

Jesus Christ, has ever lived a sinless life. The unfairness is that salvation for all nations has been extended to a humanity that is not entitled to it. None of us deserves salvation; it is only by God's goodness that salvation is made available to anyone (Rom. 3:23–25).

THE UNIVERSALISM OBJECTION

Objection: "All religions basically say the same thing; we should be good people, treat others well, and seek after God. All roads lead to the top of the same mountain, so why get caught up arguing one belief system over another?"

Response: A survey of world religions demonstrates irreconcilable differences between Christianity and other religions. There are contradictory claims, for example, between the teaching of Christianity in the Bible and Islam in the Quran about the divinity of Christ. Christ cannot be both the fully divine second person of the Trinity, as Scripture teaches, and merely a human prophet, as the Quran teaches. Ultimately, Jesus alone is sovereign over all false gods; every knee will bow to Him alone (Phil. 2:9–11).

THE INCLUSIVISM OBJECTION

Objection: "Salvation is made possible by Jesus Christ, but He has provided avenues other than specific and conscious belief in Christ as a way for salvation. All salvation ultimately leads to Christ, but there are other avenues by which people who have never heard and are genuinely seeking God may be saved and eventually come to worship Him in heaven."

Response: The testimony of Scripture is this: "It is appointed for man to die once and after that comes judgment" (Heb. 9:27). Further, the picture of the lost person who seeks after God is not one who is saved apart from Christ, but needs the revealed knowledge of Christ (Acts 10–11). It is a sobering yet Christ-exalting teaching of the Bible that humanity faces eternal judgment, and this teaching should motivate us to give our lives entirely to Him now.

Viewpoint	The sinless life, death, and resurrection of Jesus is the only means to atone for sin	Personal and specific faith in Jesus Christ is the only way to obtain that salvation
Inclusivism	Yes	No
Universalism	No	No
Biblical Christianity (Exclusivism)	Yes	Yes

THE JUDGMENTAL OBJECTION

Objections: "Christians are judgmental to think they have the only answer about God and salvation. It is overly closed-minded to think a majority of the world is going to hell forever because they do not believe in Jesus Christ, especially when so many have never heard of Him."

Response: Christians do not intend any judgmental attitude and extend the message of forgiveness in Christ because evangelism is the loving thing to do. Ultimately, it is not Christians who are passing judgment on others for their spiritual beliefs. Still, as followers of Christ, we serve as ambassadors for the message God has communicated about the consequences of sin for humanity and His loving extension of salvation in Jesus Christ (2 Cor. 5:20).

THE AGNOSTIC OBJECTION

Objection: "We do not ultimately know what happens to those who have never heard about Jesus Christ. We agree salvation is made possible by Jesus Christ, but we just don't know enough about how God responds to those who might genuinely seek Him and live good lives even though they have not heard of Jesus Christ."

Response: This objection does not take seriously the passages in Scripture that communicate humanity is spiritually dead

Exclusivity

apart from Christ and that salvation comes specifically through faith in Christ. For example, consider Ephesians 2, where those apart from Christ are described as "dead" and "children of wrath." Yet, by faith, "in Christ Jesus, you who were once far off have been brought near by the blood of Christ" (Eph. 2:13). The New Testament clearly describes the spiritual condition of humanity apart from Christ.

Conclusion

In the late nineteenth century, famed students from Cambridge University, known today as "The Cambridge Seven," sparked fervor for missions by yielding their lives to the God of the nations during their college years. Included in this group was prominent British athlete C.T. Studd. When Studd engaged the message of Scripture and the lostness of the unreached, he reoriented all of his gifts and abilities from athletic success to the priority of God's agenda. Studd and his classmates serve as an example of what is possible when college students connect the exclusivity of the gospel and the state of the unreached to a burden for taking the gospel to the nations.

This biblical teaching on the exclusivity of Christ and the desperate spiritual need of our world raises a question: what will you do with this reality? Consider these three steps of action:

- Know and treasure the work of Christ in your own life daily and deeply.
- Start sharing the message of the gospel with your friends and family right where you are. Seek to broaden your circle of relationships to include more people who do not now know Jesus. Then, deepen your friendship with them to put the love of Christ on display and compel them to believe in Christ.
- Join a healthy local church to participate in the movement of God to multiply churches among the nations.

Just as the dual realities of salvation in Jesus Christ alone and the desperate situation of the unreached peoples worldwide led the Cambridge Seven to mobilize to reach the nations, the Lord is raising up college students today. College is a time to connect your church life and future career to a burden for those who have never believed or heard the name of Jesus. Just as C.T. Studd stated, may the heartbeat of our cry be, "If Jesus Christ be God and died for me, then no sacrifice can be too great for me to make for Him."[4]

Reflection Questions

1. How does the exclusivity of Christ demonstrate the beauty of Christ?
2. What objections to the exclusivity of Christ do you wrestle with the most? What biblical passages speak to those concerns?
3. What influence should the exclusivity of Christ have on your involvement in evangelism and missions?
4. How can you take steps in your church, community, and school to support the spread of the gospel?

---

4. J.I. Packer and Mark Dever, *In My Place Condemned He Stood: Celebrating the Glory of the Atonement* (Wheaton: Crossway, 2007), 110.

Part 4

Christian Relationships and Dating

16

Friendship

How do I build strong friendships?

The most mundane things in life can become joyous moments because we are with a friend. Road trips with endless miles of driving become a fascinating combination of random humor, playlist genius, and heart-to-heart conversations. Somehow, despite the flashes of friendship that make life lighter, forging deep connections and establishing healthy friendships is elusive. The world recognizes the need for something different in our day and time. Consider this May 3, 2023, advisory on loneliness as an epidemic by the U.S. Surgeon General, Dr. Vivek Murthy:

> Our epidemic of loneliness and isolation has been an underappreciated public health crisis that has harmed individual and societal health. Our relationships are a source of healing and well-being hiding in plain sight – one that can help us live healthier, more fulfilled, and more productive lives[.][1]

More classically, Shakespeare famously said the following, conveying friendship's importance and the value of permanence:

---

1. Vivek Murthy, New Surgeon General Advisory Raises Alarm about the Devastating Impact of the Epidemic of Loneliness and Isolation in the United States, https://www.hhs.gov/about/news/2023/05/03/new-surgeon-general-advisory-raises-alarm-about-devastating-impact-epidemic-loneliness-isolation-united-states.html. Accessed 23 July 2024.

> Those friends thou hast, and their adoption tried,
> Grapple them to thy soul with hoops of steel.[2]

Friendship is not just about sentimental notions from poets or the societal benefits of fighting loneliness. The Surgeon General and Shakespeare value friendship because God designed each of us to enjoy friendship. Consider the following biblical foundations for friendship. The roots for all friendship are found in God's nature. God's nature as Trinity is that He is eternally in joyful fellowship with Himself as Father, Son, and Spirit. Flowing from God's nature to us as His creation is the fact that we are made for friendship. We are created in God's image, which includes a reflection of God's relational nature in our nature. Remarkably, our significance in life touches on the notion of friendship. The purpose of our existence is friendship (with God). God's purpose in creating humanity was to enjoy Him in open and unhindered relationships (Exod. 33:11). It is no surprise that one description of our salvation is that we are made friends with God (John 15:13-15; James 2:23). The relational nature of God toward us as His image-bearing creatures is experienced in salvation.

When it comes to friendships between people, the Bible offers rich resources. Resulting from the fact that all humanity bears God's image, friendship has a unique dynamic. Augustine notes friendship between people – whether toward a believer or an unbeliever – always involves God in the middle. He stated: "They love their friends truly who love God in them, either because God is already in them, or in order that God might be in them."[3] In addition to these theological roots for friendship, the Bible offers significant instruction about friendship (Prov. 12:16; 13:20; 17:17; 18:24; 27:6, 17; Eccles. 4:9–12). Finally, we cannot be effective disciple-makers without friendship. One way of defining disciple-making is *teaching the truth in the context of friendship.* Consider Jesus'

---

2. William Shakespeare, *Hamlet* (New York: Washington Square Press, 2004), 43.

3. Augustine, Sermon 361.1, "Augustine on Friendship." *AUGNET*, www.augnet. org/en/works-of-augustine/his-ideas/2311-augustine-on-friendship/. Accessed 23 July 2024.

Friendship

example of lived relationship with His disciples and Paul's description of His love for the church in 1 Thessalonians.

Needless to say, friendship is all over the Bible. No wonder friendship is such a joy when it is good and so painful when it is corrupted. One fascinating thing most people don't know is that many noted theologians wrote about friendship. St. Augustine was the most prolific. Here's a taste of his teaching about friendship:

> Particularly when I am worn out by the upsets of the world, I cast myself without reservation on the love of those who are especially close to me. I know I can safely entrust my thoughts and considerations to those who are aflame with Christian love and have become faithful friends to me. For I am entrusting them not to another human, but to God in Whom they dwell and by Whom they are who they are (*Letter* 73,3).

Another famous theologian, J.C. Ryle, is noted for saying, "Friendship halves our troubles—and doubles our joys!"[4]

So, we know this: 1) Friendship is important. 2) We struggle with it uniquely in our day and time. 3) We cannot fulfill the Great Commission without friendship. 4) God has wisdom to help us figure it out so we can enjoy Him as we edify one another. These are the reasons why the following habits are worth exploring.

What are the foundations of friendship?

The first step to cultivating joyful and fruitful friendships is to know what friendship is and treat it accordingly. The biblical summary of friendship above shows that friendship is not a consumer relationship meant to make us feel good. It is an opportunity to reflect God's nature to the world, treat others the way God treats them, find joy in deep relationships, and positively influence others. The oxygen is taken out of friendship by a consumer mentality that thinks of friends

---

4.   J.C. Ryle, *"The Best Friend," Practical Religion* (Edinburgh: Banner of Truth Trust, 2013), 317.

through the lens of "what have you done for me lately." Friends are not to be viewed transactionally or as a means to some other end. God does not view us that way as He invites us into a relationship with Him, and so our thinking about others should be oriented the same way.

Knowing that friendship is for beautiful and meaningful purposes, the orientation of how we think about it changes. The first step to good friendships is to train our thinking about it according to what it is. Friendship is not a consumer relationship but a mutual fellowship and upbuilding of profound significance. Switching this orientation will result in prioritizing friendship and prioritizing others in a way that glorifies God.

> A man of many companions may come to ruin, but there is a friend who sticks closer than a brother (Prov. 18:24).

How do I choose friends?

The Bible, as well as personal experience, instructs us to choose our closest friends wisely. In a time when social media gives the impression we have dozens (if not hundreds or thousands) of "friends," it can become confusing what and with whom our actual relationships are. Moreover, it's an assumed virtue not to exclude anyone, so our networks become wide and shallow. We should certainly be friendly with everyone in our proximity. At the same time, not every relationship is meant to operate at the same depth.

An often overlooked dynamic is that our friends are a unique influence on us. Show us your five closest friends, and we can predict the kind of person you will be in a few years' time. Wise friendship requires going the deepest with those who are the wisest influences upon us. Beyond your deepest friendships, you can continue to be in relationships with others and influence them. The posture will be different, and time will tell whether those relationships will go deeper or trail off.

Friendship

Whoever walks with the wise becomes wise, but the companion of fools will suffer harm (Prov. 13:20).

BE PATIENT AND COMMITTED

Friendships take time to form. Sometimes, they take a painfully long time. You might feel as though you are trying so hard and still cannot find the kind of friends you desire. In addition, technology-driven factors limit how much time people spend with one another. This means that friendships are formed slowly and with much commitment. Friendships are not instantly replicated on a 3D printer. They are forged through the ups and downs of life. As we pursue deeper friendships, we must also trust God's timing. If we do not have the disposition to trust God's timing, we can tend toward grasping too tightly to a relationship or feeling the controlling need to orchestrate a relationship. Exhibit patience to keep pursuing friendship even when it feels like it does not gain momentum naturally. Remain committed through the difficult times as well as the good times. Friendship endures all seasons, and sometimes, establishing friendship must do the same.

A friend loves at all times, and a brother is born for adversity (Prov. 17:17).

LOVE BY BEARING AND FORGIVING

My (Jon's) youngest two kids have what seems to be a unique and close friendship as siblings. There's constant mutual entertainment and antics when they are with each other. It's almost difficult to think of one without the other. Given all the wonderful qualities of their relationship, they can also oscillate in a matter of moments between the best of sibling friendship to each other's greatest annoyance. As it is with siblings, so it is with voluntary friends. No matter how wonderful the character and chemistry between friends, the relationship is still between imperfect people.

This is where the gospel ingredients of bearing with one another and forgiving one another enter. Bearing with one another is recognizing there are different preferences between people. Eighty percent of life preferences might overlap with a close friend, but the other twenty percent may not. The difference is not bad in that twenty percent, but it is the opportunity to bear with differences between people. Bearing with one another also means demonstrating patience for people to grow. A friend might have weaknesses and be seeking to work on those flaws. Without excusing sin, demonstrate patience because spiritual transformation happens over time. In other instances, friendship calls for forgiveness and reconciliation rather than forbearance. When one person sins against another, the correct response is confessing that sin, seeking reconciliation, and granting forgiveness. Practice forgiveness in your friendships as one who has received much forgiveness. Love that bears with others patiently and forgives eagerly is critical to joy-filled friendships.

> Put on then, as God's chosen ones, holy and beloved, compassionate hearts, kindness, humility, meekness, and patience, bearing with one another and, if one has a complaint against another, forgiving each other; as the Lord has forgiven you, so you also must forgive (Col. 3:12-13).

IN-PERSON RELATIONSHIPS

Research by sociologists Jonathan Haidt and Jean Twenge shows a critical impact on Generation Z in that personal relationships have diminished in favor of digital interactions.[5] All the various manifestations of social media and messaging have resulted in a net result of far more hours interacting with a screen and far fewer in person than any previous generation. The impact of this shift is both individual and collective. Individually, anxiety and depression have skyrocketed. Collectively, students arrive at college uncertain of how to

---

5. Haidt, Jonathan, *The Anxious Generation: How the Great Rewiring of Childhood is Causing an Epidemic of Mental Illness* (New York: Penguin Press, 2024); Twenge, Jean, *Generations: The Real Differences Between Gen Z, Millennials, Gen X, Boomers, and Silents – and what they mean for America's Future* (New York: Atria Books, 2023).

Friendship

navigate the social interactions that a residential college experience brings.

Counter this cultural current by prioritizing in-person relationships. Create a rhythm of life by eating meals together, going on coffee runs, working out with friends, going to concerts, or any other activity you find interesting. Put the phones away when you are with each other and enjoy the moment. While all our smart devices have many wonderful benefits, do not allow them to fragment your friendship capacity. Sometimes, friends with us in person are even better than a beloved family member hundreds of miles away. Presence matters.

> Oil and perfume make the heart glad, and the sweetness of a friend comes from his earnest counsel. Do not forsake your friend and your father's friend, and do not go to your brother's house in the day of your calamity. Better is a neighbor who is near than a brother who is far away (Prov. 27:9-10).

CARE WITH WORDS

Words have the power to build up and the power to tear down. The closer the relationship, the more power a person's words have in our lives. Unwise words and the sins of gossip and slander have devastated many friendships. We should not only proactively avoid sinful speech patterns. We should also be mindful of empty joking, sarcasm that is intended playfully but could hurt another, and breaking confidence with sensitive information. Speak truth to one another and about one another. Season speech with charity. Avoid sharing through the friend group what you heard about another that may or may not be edifying. Talk to one another about friction more than you talk about one another to other people. Embrace habits of wise speech, find others who do the same, and friendship building will be much more enjoyable.

> The heart of the wise makes his speech judicious and adds persuasiveness to his lips. Gracious words are like a honeycomb, sweetness to the soul and health to the body (Prov. 16:23–24).

A dishonest man spreads strife, and a whisperer separates close friends (Prov. 16:28).

Conclusion

Friends build one another up through encouraging, warning, and supporting. Friendship should be characterized by communicating in ways that build the other up. Encouraging involves sharing the truths of Scripture, showing up for competitions and performances, complimenting positive attributes, and cheering one another on. Every one of us also takes steps astray and has blind spots to our own character weaknesses. Faithful friends press through the relationship discomfort of speaking difficult truth. Warning involves lovingly and humbly helping a friend understand their wrong and encouraging them to turn toward Jesus. Finally, friends build one another up through unfailing support. Life will bring many trials. When suffering comes, the friend who sticks with you will have a special place in your life. We have the opportunity to do the same for others.

> And we urge you, brothers, admonish the idle, encourage the fainthearted, help the weak, be patient with them all (1 Thess. 5:14).

> Faithful are the wounds of a friend; profuse are the kisses of an enemy (Prov. 27:6).

> Two are better than one, because they have a good reward for their toil. For if they fall, one will lift up his fellow. But woe to him who is alone when he falls and has not another to lift him up! (Eccles. 4:9-10).

Friendship is magnificent because it is created by God, manifests His character in everyday ways, and brings deep blessings. Entrust yourself to the Lord as your chief friend. Then, strive toward becoming a good friend to others. May the Lord supply you with many good friends along the way.

Reflection Questions

1. Who in your life has proven to be a good friend, and what qualities do you appreciate about that person?
2. If someone observed your interactions with friends for a month, what would they conclude about how you value and treat your friends?
3. Which habits can you implement in your current friendships to help foster growth?
4. Sould you seek reconciliation with any current or former friends for how you have treated them?

17

Dating

What is the purpose of dating?

A fifth grader comes home and declares to his mom, "I am dating a girl in my science class." She remains calm and responds, "Does that mean you are going on dates?" "Well, no. That's not what dating means," he replies. She questions, "Well, what do you mean by dating?" In this scenario, the mother and the fifth grader have different expectations about dating. At this point, it probably will not be too challenging for her to instruct him about what dating should and should not be.

However, the issue gets more complicated when the fifth grader ages, and the nature of dating remains undefined. What the fifth grader means by dating is probably different from what the fifteen-year-old means, and different from what the freshman in college means. We tend to operate at each of these stages with certain assumptions about what dating is and is not. In many modern cultures, the practice of dating is taken for granted, even though people mean vastly different things when they say "we're dating." Then there are also finer distinctions in dating terminology, such as "dating exclusively" or "dating around." Dating often involves tremendous pressure, expense, and time, but it is essential to place dating in its proper context.

It used to be assumed that dating was a prequel to marriage, but now, the practice of dating might have nothing at all to do with marriage. We want to state at the outset that dating without a view toward marriage mistakes what dating should be about. Further, even if Christians and non-Christians share a similar goal in dating (i.e., finding someone to marry), their manner of pursuing this goal is radically different. This difference in pursuit is partly due to them defining a "successful" marriage in often radically different ways. Dating has a derived importance: dating is important because marriage is important. Dating is important because it leads to something greater: the covenant of marriage.

What is dating?

Someone has joked that the sum total of what the Bible has to say about dating would fit on the front and back of a blank sheet of paper. On one level, that statement is correct. As you have read the Bible, you did not accidentally read over the chapters about dating. The Bible does describe people in the early stages of their relationships. Think of Isaac and Rebekah, Boaz and Ruth, David and Abigail, or Joseph and Mary. However, these stories are primarily descriptive of the practices of the day and do not translate exactly to our modern practice. The term "dating" is not in the Bible. So, dating is not formally commanded of Christians. In fact, many marriages among Christians have not been preceded by the couple dating; instead, their marriages have been arranged by families. But to say that the word "dating" is not present in the Bible does not mean that the Bible has nothing to say about the concept. Dating, as we use the term today, was not a common cultural practice in the ancient world. That fact, however, does not mean that dating is an unbiblical practice, but it does mean that we need to be careful to define its goals and practices in light of important biblical concepts.

Because dating's importance is derived from the importance of marriage, dating's goal must be defined by marriage. Someone might object to this by suggesting that dating can be

Dating

used more generally as just hanging out as friends without any romantic inclinations or intentions of marriage. That's fine, but we would caution Christians to use a different term (perhaps the term "friendship") to distinguish from the common cultural definition of dating to include romantic intentions. In another chapter, we have defined marriage as a gracious covenant before God between a man and a woman in order to establish public order, enable procreation, bring pleasure to spouses, and provide a picture of Christ's love for the church. The goal of dating is the pursuit of that kind of God-honoring relationship. Thus, dating is spending intentional time with someone to discern God's call to marriage or singleness, and if marriage, to that particular person or not. This definition presupposes that most Christians will get married, but it also acknowledges that some will be single (1 Cor. 7:7–8). Secondly, if the Christian discerns that he or she should pursue marriage, the question becomes "to whom?" In reality, these two questions (Marriage or not? To whom?) are often discerned simultaneously. Perhaps the word that will be most overlooked in this definition is "discernment." The practice of dating gets confused when it is not about pursuing clarity in decision-making.

What is the goal of dating?

How many times have we heard of a young lady searching for Mr. Right? The goal of the search is to find the right someone to marry. Or how many times have you heard a friend claim that she just wants to have a wedding? And sometimes, on college campuses, there is the added pressure of a "ring by Spring." If you haven't heard of the last one, you might be better off for it. Each of these scenarios has expressed specific goals for their dating endeavors. But are these the right goals?

Dating is about discernment.[1] Thus, the goal of dating is clarity. Is the person whom you are dating a person

---

1. For carefully parsing the difference between intimacy and clarity, I am indebted to Marshall Segal, *Not Yet Married: The Pursuit of Joy in Singleness and Dating* (Wheaton, IL: Crossway, 2007).

with whom you could have a God-honoring marriage in a reasonably short amount of time?[2] If the answer is no, then stop dating. If the answer is yes, then start moving toward marriage. If the answer is unclear, then keep seeking clarity through prayer and counsel, and perhaps keep dating. This all assumes that marriage is a good institution that should be pursued. Marriage does have limitations (Matt. 22:30; Mark 12:25; 1 Cor. 7:25–40), but it has been God's good design from the beginning of creation (Gen. 2:18–25). Marriage is to "be held in honor among all" (Heb. 13:4) and not forbidden or downgraded (1 Tim. 4:3). Dating without some dreams of marriage is a skewed endeavor.

We will cover what to look for in a potential spouse in another chapter, but it bears saying more than once that a Christian should be looking for someone who is a maturing Christian. Paul's counsel for those seeking to marry is that Christians are free to pursue marriage "only in the Lord" (1 Cor. 7:39; cf. 2 Cor. 6:14). That is, Paul's stipulation for a Christian seeking to be married is that he or she seek another Christian to marry. This stipulation makes sense when the ultimate goal of marriage is understood to have a marriage that spotlights Christ's love (Eph. 5:22–33).

If the goal of dating is to pursue clarity in decision-making, there are some implications for how one dates. For example, boundaries help in decision-making. By way of comparison, a judge who has an economic interest in the results of a legal decision is ethically called to recuse himself from the decision. The assumption is that blurring the boundaries between financial gain and justice could cloud one's judgment. Similarly, when Christians pursue intimacy in dating, it clouds

---

2. We recognize that the phrase "reasonably short amount of time" could be frustratingly vague. Life circumstances are varied enough that it prevents us from giving too much more specificity. A young man and a young lady in their late twenties who have been serving alongside one another in church for some time might be wise to pursue marriage more quickly than the nineteen-year-olds who met recently. The first couple has had time to discern the character of the other through their shared ministry. Moreover, their life circumstances are ready for marriage. They would come to the relationship with clarity about their deep-seated beliefs, desires, and dreams.

their ability to pursue clarity. Marshall Segal counsels, "A lot of the heartache and confusion we feel in dating stems from treating dating mainly as practice for marriage (clarity *through* intimacy), instead of discernment toward marriage (clarity *and then* intimacy)."[3] If clarity is the goal, Christians might be wise to limit emotional connections while dating. That is not to say that emotional connection is forbidden, but too quick and too deep of an emotional connection will cloud one's clarity of discernment. If clarity is the goal, Christians are wise to limit physical contact in dating. Again, that doesn't mean that all physical contact is categorically forbidden. Demonstrate to your "future spouse" that you reserve physical intimacy for the marriage union. Single "you" will be the married "you." Expressions of sexual, physical contact should be reserved for marriage, but there could be expressions of physical touch that may be acceptable for a dating couple.

What are some dangers of misunderstanding the goal of dating?

Given the goal of dating for the Christian (i.e., to seek clarity), it might be helpful to cover a few common concepts about dating. The counsel we provide arises from decades of serving in college and young adult ministries. We have attempted to provide biblical wisdom to these cultural practices.

FLIRTATION

Admittedly, this term can be used in a spectrum of ways in our culture. If by "flirtation," someone means a smile that indicates romantic interest, then that might be the precursor to intentional dating. The *Cambridge Dictionary*, however, describes flirtation in a different way: "a situation in which someone behaves as if sexually attracted to another person, without being seriously interested."[4] It is hard to see how this behavior is consistent with a Christian approach to dating.

---

3. Segal, *Not Yet Married*, 140.

4. Accessed March 15, 2024: https://dictionary.cambridge.org/us/dictionary/english/flirtation.

The goal of this type of flirtation is to stroke one's own ego as being recognized by another as sexually desirable. But the flirter has no real intention of pursuing dating or marriage. Thus, the flirtatious person is lying about his or her intentions.

MISSIONARY DATING

In Christian circles, "missionary dating" is sometimes used to describe the practice of a Christian dating a non-Christian in the hopes that the non-Christian will convert to the Christian faith. With the definition of dating we have provided, it is no surprise that we would not recommend this foolish practice. This practice is tied up with pursuing intimacy, romance, or emotional connection rather than clarity. If we are to marry "only in the Lord" and dating is about discerning fitness for marriage, then dating also should be "in the Lord."[5]

DATING EXCLUSIVELY

The practice of dating exclusively can be defined by its adverb "exclusively." It is contrasted with the practice of dating multiple people simultaneously.[6] It is wise to have a number of friendships, but it is not wise to have a number of dating relationships. It would be a challenge to discern with clarity multiple simultaneous relationships. Our counsel is to date one person at a time. When you have clarity about that relationship, either move forward or move on.

DISCERNING FOR YOURSELF BY YOURSELF

The pressure and emotion of dating sometimes make discernment more challenging. That is where the church

---

5. There is a difference between a dating relationship and a marriage between a Christian and a non-Christian. In a marriage, the Christian should remain in the covenant relationship even if it is with a non-Christian (1 Cor. 7:12–14) in the hopes that the person will convert (1 Pet. 3:1–2). The Christian has entered into a valid covenant relationship, and the Christian must be faithful to that covenant. But in a dating relationship, there has been no covenant commitment. The Christian should leave that dating relationship because that relationship will not result in a marriage that is "in the Lord."

6. Some also define "dating exclusively" as a lesser status than a "relationship."

and family can help. The Bible says, "The way of a fool is right in his own eyes, but a wise man listens to advice" (Prov. 12:15). Listening to Christian counsel is an important part of practicing wise discernment. The prayerful perspective of wise Christian friends and family provides another perspective that you might not be able to see at the moment. Sometimes, couples ask their pastor to officiate at their wedding and their parents to be excited about the marriage (and often pay for the wedding) while they remove them from any role in the pre-marriage process. This does not honor either the pastor or the parents. Even more, it robs a couple of significant Christian counsel from those who love them most deeply.

ONLINE DATING

We will not say that online dating is categorically prohibited, but the final stages of discernment require more face-to-face interaction. Online profiles lend themselves to a projection of what people want to be true of themselves or what they want others to think is true about them. However, these projections do not always correspond to reality. Because marriage is not an online relationship, it is wise that dating not be exclusively an online relationship. It is also helpful to observe firsthand a person's interactions with others, especially in the church and family. But online dating might be an effective way to meet someone with whom to pursue a dating relationship. So online platforms might be a place to meet someone, but they are not sufficient to discern whether or not to marry someone.

Conclusion

Dating is hard. And dating can make one feel very vulnerable. When a dating relationship ends, sometimes people feel that they have been rejected. But if the purpose of dating is the pursuit of clarity, then breaking up is not bad. Breaking up provides clarity, even if you had hoped that clarity would be in a different direction. Again, dating's meaning is tied up with the meaning of marriage. And when a godly marriage (or singleness) is the goal of dating, then the practice of dating becomes clearer.

Reflection Questions

1. How have you heard people express the purpose of dating?
2. How does your understanding of the purpose of dating influence how you think about dating relationships?
3. What are some common missteps or unwise practices that you observe in the practice of dating?
4. If you are currently in a relationship, are there adjustments you need to make?

18

Marriage

What is marriage?

Rarely does any culture's valuation of marriage begin to rise to the level of the Bible's valuation of marriage. The Bible begins (Adam and Eve) and ends (Christ and the Church) with marriage.[1] Between these marriage bookends, marriage and its effects are interwoven into many pages of Scripture. It is a central and significant biblical theme. But marriage is also less than some people describe it. Marriage is not ultimate, and marriage does not "complete you." Marriage is secondary to the ultimate realities of God's glory and Christ's love for the church. One pastor describes marriage like this: "The ultimate thing we can say about marriage is that it exists for God's glory. That is, it exists to display God. Now we see how: Marriage is patterned after Christ's covenant relationship to his redeemed people, the church. And therefore, the highest meaning and the most ultimate purpose of marriage is to put the covenant relationship of Christ and his church on display. That is why marriage exists."[2] So marriage is extremely important but not ultimately important—even the best human marriages do not extend into eternity.

---

1. I first read this observation in Tim Keller, *The Meaning of Marriage: Facing the Complexities of Commitment with the Wisdom of God* (New York: Dutton, 2011), 13.

2. John Piper, *This Momentary Marriage: A Parable of Permanence* (Wheaton: Crossway, 2009), 25.

How does the Bible present marriage?

God created the glorious stars, delicate flowers, and intricate animals, then declared it all good. Perhaps the most remarkable aspect of creation, at this point, is that in all this created goodness, God pointed out something that was incomplete. At the end of each creation day, God declared things to be good. But "Then the LORD God said, 'It is not good that man should be alone; I will make a helper fit for him'" (Gen. 2:18). God created Eve by using a part of Adam, not because God could not have created her without Adam's rib, but so that God could teach us about the created intention for marriage: "Therefore a man shall leave his father and his mother and hold fast to his wife, and they shall become one flesh" (Gen. 2:24). Even this explanation of marriage is prospective because there were not yet parents from whom to leave. Remarkably, the foundational relationship God creates is the husband and the wife, not other good relationships like the parent-child or between siblings. Those relationships will flow out of the marriage relationship. Even their commission to "be fruitful and multiply" depends on their marriage union.

Adam and Eve's marital bliss, along with the rest of created bliss, did not last long. By the time we turn to the third chapter of the Bible, this married couple has fallen into sin. Instead of this union reinforcing their mutual commitment to and love for God, the temptation to doubt God's goodness takes root in their hearts as Adam fails to chart a course of faithfulness. As a consequence of this rebellion, the beautiful complementarity of this union will continually be under attack as God reports to the woman, "Your desire shall be contrary to your husband, but he shall rule over you" (Gen. 3:16). From this point forward, marriage is a mixture of God's blessing and the challenge of sin.

Many of the marriages in Genesis involve grievous failures that teach us about the brokenness of the world and God's grace amid human unfaithfulness. The lingering implications of the Fall are evident in Abraham and Sarah's marriage through their inability to conceive children. Marriage is created to

Marriage

result in fruitfulness, but even physical intimacy and its fruits are affected by the Fall. When their marriage does not produce offspring, Abraham and Sarah take matters into their own hands and distort marriage even further by Abraham having a child with another woman—this plan to operate outside of God's good bounds results in further heartache. We begin to see a pattern develop: redefining marriage results in terrible heartache. Isaac and Rebekah's marriage is far from ideal, as she manipulates him through Jacob. Similarly, Jacob's polygamous marriages result in competition and heartache to the extent that his wives barter for his sexual intimacy.

Flipping through the pages of the rest of Scripture, we see the goodness of marriage, its perversion by humanity, and its protection by God. In the Law, God prescribes ways to protect and uphold marriage as a foundational union on which society is structured (e.g., Exod. 20:14; Deut. 20:7). We might expect the kings of Israel to be examples of upholding God's standards, but in reality, they tended to be some of the worst violators of God's ideals for marriage. The Israelite kings were characterized by multiplying wives, entering unions for the wrong reasons, and being led into false worship by these unions.

Reflecting on some of this perversion and seeking to restore God's good design, the wisdom books have much to say about marriage. The Book of Proverbs warns against adultery and correspondingly celebrates marital physical intimacy: "Let your fountain be blessed, and rejoice in the wife of your youth, a lovely deer, a graceful doe. Let her breasts fill you at all times with delight; be intoxicated always in her love" (Prov. 5:18–19). The text communicates a biblical view of marriage that is for procreation (i.e., "fountain be blessed") and for pleasure ("rejoice," "delight," "be intoxicated"). On the contrary, Proverbs warns several times about the heartache of deviating from God's plan for marriage: "It is better to live in the corner of a housetop than in a house shared with a quarrelsome wife" (Prov. 21:9). The wise instruction about marriage culminates in Proverbs 31 that describes the wise woman who is a joy and delight to her husband. The Song of Solomon graphically describes marital love. Some argue that this description is a metaphor for God's love while others take it at face value as a literal description of marital love. Regardless of the interpretation, the view of marriage is positive, and physical intimacy within marriage is viewed positively.

There is a remarkable shift in the way marriage is described in the prophetic books. Instead of speaking of the created goodness of marriage, the prophetic books tend to focus on the brokenness of marriage, heartache, and adulterous betrayal. And they use this tragedy of human marriage to describe how the people betrayed their relationship with God. The readers know both the joy that marriage should be and the heartache that it often is. Isaiah 1:21 (see also Jeremiah 2:20–24) laments how Israel has forsaken a covenant relationship with God: "How the faithful city has become a whore, she who was full of justice! Righteousness lodged in her, but now murderers." Other texts like Ezekiel 16 and the Book of Hosea continue this imagery of idolatry being compared to adultery.

While Jesus never married, He held high the covenant of marriage, even performing His first miracle at a wedding feast (John 2). In Matthew 19, He corrects some of the abuses of marriage and reinforces the lifelong commitment that God has always intended for marriage. His emphasis on the lifetime permanence of marriage begins to hint at what Paul will develop more fully in his Epistles that human marriage pictures the divine marriage between Christ and the church, which has eternal permanence. Paul reinforces the goodness of marriage and physical intimacy and bases that on the theology of the goodness of the material body. In 1 Corinthians 7, he instructs the church that singleness has great value in being freer for ministry, but not everyone has the gift of singleness; in fact, many have the gift of marriage, and married couples should give themselves to one another physically. Similar to Paul's instructions for wives to submit and husbands to lead lovingly, 1 Peter 3 provides instructions for husbands and wives.

Human marriage is not everlasting. In Luke 20:27–36, Jesus explains that there will be no marriage at the resurrection. Why? Well, the purposes of marriage are transformed. Procreation will be unnecessary. Pleasure will be escalated to be life with God, and companionship will be fulfilled in that life with God. Perhaps the most significant text for understanding the ultimate meaning of marriage is Ephesians 5 in which Paul explains human marriage as pointing to a greater and deeper spiritual reality: Christ's love for the church.

As a Christian, how should I think about marriage?

The pervasive cultural redefinition of marriage has created some confusion about marriage in the church. We are not suggesting that at some time in the past the prevailing cultural view of marriage aligned perfectly with a biblical view of marriage; instead, we are observing that the rapid redefinition of long-established institutions like marriage by the broader culture can have an impact on the way that Christians think about these institutions. The section above presented how the Bible describes marriage. Now it is helpful to synthesize some of these texts into a coherent understanding of Christian marriage.

Marriage is a gracious covenant before God between a man and woman in order to establish public order, enable procreation, bring pleasure to spouses, and provide a picture of Christ's love for the church. The first thing to note is that marriage is a gracious gift of God. God established the first marriage between Adam and Eve. The covenantal nature of marriage is a recognition that God established this union and that the commitments that a husband and a wife make to one another are made first and foremost before God. For nearly two millennia, Christians have univocally affirmed the complementarity of one man and one woman in marriage. Despite recent cultural redefinitions, the biblical testimony is clear and unchanging that God intends marriage to be exclusively focused on another person, between a man and woman.

When God established the marriage relationship, He established it to fulfill several purposes: public order, pleasure, procreation, and picturing. Firstly, God instituted marriage as the foundational unit to order society, provide stability, and enable human flourishing. In Genesis 2:24, we read about the first marriage: "Therefore a man shall leave his father and his mother and hold fast to his wife, and they shall become one flesh."

Secondly, God intends marriage for pleasure. The enjoyment of marriage is not primarily physical; marriage is about a deeper pleasure of relationship and union. Proverbs 5 instructs a husband to "rejoice in the wife of your youth." Then, the Bible describes both the relational and physical joy of marriage. God intends marriage for human enjoyment and pleasure!

Third, God intends marriage for procreation. In Genesis 1, we read that God blessed the man and woman and commanded them to "be fruitful and multiply." God commissions Adam and Eve to come together to produce offspring. That's the first task with which they are entrusted. And it's only within marriage that God sanctions sexual activity. While not every marriage results in children, it is a good disposition for marriages to be open to children. And Christians should view children as blessings from the Lord and desire them.

Finally, marriage ultimately is about picturing the redemptive love of the covenant-keeping God. God created marriage to teach us about Him. Because marriage is so special and so intimate, God uses it as an image or picture to describe something even more important. Marriage is something symbolic; it exists, in part, to draw attention to something greater than itself. Ephesians 5 says, "Husbands, love your wives, as Christ loved the church and gave himself up for her..." (Eph 5:25). Marriage, as it is intended to function, should be a picture of Christ's love for the church in the way that husbands lovingly serve, sacrifice for, and lead their wives. The Bible is not unaware of the challenges of marriage or how marriage is practiced wrongly; on the contrary, the Bible often describes the pain that results from not seeking God's way in marriage. Nevertheless, God intends marriage to be for our good now and to point us to the ultimate goal of life with him.

Conclusion

Marriage is a good thing. But here are two frequent questions that younger Christians ask: "Is the desire to be married a good thing?" "And is the desire for children a good thing?" The answer to both of these questions is "yes." Desiring marriage and desiring children are good desires, even though both must be kept in their proper places. The Apostle Paul indicates in 1 Corinthians 7 that God calls some Christians to singleness, so marriage must not become an absolute desire. Christians must understand both marriage and singleness as ways to glorify God.

Reflection Questions:

1. What are some godly motivations for pursuing marriage? Could you think of some insufficient or ungodly reasons that people pursue marriage?
2. What are the essential qualities of a God-honoring marriage?
3. What are some similarities and dissimilarities between a biblical view of marriage and common cultural views of marriage?
4. Are there further questions that you have about marriage? Is there someone in your church which with whom you could talk?

19

Discernment 1

How do I know when I am ready to date?

Backcountry camping is a liberating experience. Setting out with everything you need to escape crowds, electronics, and the compression of everyday life brings life to the soul. The outdoors may not be your cup of tea, but take our word for it. Finding a beautiful spot in nature where it's you and a few of your close friends or family does wonders for our souls. Sometimes, people new to backcountry camping overlook a critical part of the process. They do not adequately assess their readiness. Do I have all the supplies I will need? Did we pack enough food, and will we have adequate access to water? Is my gear appropriate to the climate range we will experience? Did I pack the snake bite kit?! Rightly assessing your preparedness before you start the journey is often the difference between making or breaking the experience. The same goes for dating.

How do I know if I am prepared?

We have already established that the ultimate purpose of dating is to gain discernment regarding marriage. Your first impulse might be to discern if the candidates around you are worth dating. Not so fast. Start by discerning if you are becoming the right person before focusing on finding the right person. Here are five areas to consider when evaluating if you are ready to date.

SPIRITUAL MATURITY

Do you possess basic and growing spiritual maturity? A healthy Christian life is characterized by the word "maturity." The Apostle Paul characterized the result of discipleship as maturity. He proclaimed Christ, corrected wrong ways, and taught the Scriptures to the Colossians *so that* they would be mature (Col. 1:28–29). If the purpose of discipleship for Paul's investment in the Colossians was maturity, it is a good signal that maturity should characterize the normal Christian. Hebrews 6:1 tells us to press on toward maturity. Ephesians 4:13–16 frames Christian living as growing up in Christ and attaining maturity. Maturity is defined as becoming like Christ as we grow "into him" (v. 15).

What exactly constitutes maturity? Maturity does not mean perfection. In human development, we do not argue that adolescents make mistakes, and when they mature as adults, they suddenly achieve perfection. You know that is not true of the older people in your life, even those you admire. Maturity is about the general characteristic of being Christ-like. Sinclair Ferguson's book *Maturity* describes the goal as "growing up and going on in the Christian life."[3] You may have heard the phrase "failure to launch" as a catchphrase for a twenty (or thirty) something-year-old who does not get a job, retains an immature lifestyle, fails to embrace responsibility, and lives dependently on his parents. Spiritual maturity is choosing to no longer idle in neutral spirituality but to wholeheartedly launch into ownership of pursuing Christ through faith and faithful living.

Christlikeness is a matter of the heart. As we walk with Christ, the Holy Spirit uses the Word of God to conform us to the image of Christ (2 Cor. 3:18). Transforming us from immaturity to maturity is God's supernatural work of change that results from salvation (Rom. 12:1–2). At the same time, the fact that God has the power to grow us does not mean

---

3. Sinclair Ferguson, *Maturity: Growing Up and Going On in the Christian Life* (Edinburgh: Banner of Truth Trust, 2019).

we are passive. Maturity is manifested outwardly through essential Christian habits. For example, choose the Lordship of Christ over lesser desires and preferences for life (Luke 9:23). Spend time fellowshipping with Christ in the Bible, prayer, evangelism, and local church fellowship. Pursue influencing others spiritually to help them become more like Christ (Matt. 28:18–20). Do these things characterize your life? Be sure you are "growing up and going on in the Christian life" before worrying about going on a date.

IDENTITY IN CHRIST

The concept of personal identity has exploded in our times. You are likely familiar with people who identify in all sorts of ways. The way a person identifies eventually dictates their entire way of life. Identity in Christ is modern language intended to convey an ancient reality for our times. Those who have placed their faith in Christ are chiefly identified by their union with Him. Whatever may be true of you (ethnicity, education level, personality, talents, nationality, gender, etc.) is subservient to something that is chiefly true – the fact that you are in Christ. There is an identity to rule all your other identities. Life "in Christ" is the most critical and influential reality that defines the rest of life (Gal. 2:20; 2 Cor. 5:17; Col. 3:1–4; Eph. 2:10).

We tend to have identity amnesia. We forget who ultimately defines us, and the results are messy. Identity amnesia creates significant damage in dating and marriage. We forget we are complete in Christ, so we look to the other person to complete us. We forget Christ is sufficient and provides all we need, so we quarrel in relationships to feel more secure. We forget ultimate satisfaction is in a relationship with Christ, so we pursue sinful pleasures with the other person. We forget Christ is the ultimate one, and we are not, so we overestimate our preferences and seek control. The examples of how a clear and strong identity in Christ is necessary for healthy relationships could go on. Do you know who you are in Christ and apply that truth to your life? If you are not rooted in your identity in Christ, you might seek fulfillment in another person who is not designed to provide it. Be sure you know who you are in Christ before you worry about getting to know another person on a date.

HOLINESS

God is holy. God's holiness means He is perfect and unpolluted in any way. His excellence and beauty are unsurpassable. God's purity infuses all His other attributes. His power is perfectly manifested and righteous because He is holy. His knowledge and will are pristine and without flaw because He is holy. What this ultimately means is God is entirely unlike any person or other thing He has created. What a marvelous reality about God!

Then, there's this incredible command rooted in God's holiness. God says, "Be Holy, because I am holy" (Lev. 19:2; 20:7; 20:26; 21:8; Exod. 19:6; 1 Pet. 1:16; 1 Thess. 4:7). Holiness is often thought of in relation to how much we are sinning in comparison to the people around us, and how known our sins might be. Many think they are holy because they are better off than those around them. That is the wrong standard for holiness. Compared to God, we all are in deep need of transformation. Be holy *as God* is holy. God's nature is the standard, and we are to become like Him as we walk with Him.

What does this have to do with readiness for dating? You cannot be the kind of person who will make a good husband or wife if you are not willing to live in holiness as a single man or woman. Accepted patterns of sin brought into dating will inevitably influence the other person away from Christ. Even if you hate and wrestle with it in the secret space of self-willed struggle, sin patterns will ultimately undermine healthy relationships. Like water eroding the foundation of a building, the impact may not be evident for some time as you maintain a positive outward image. Over time, the effect is devastating when, one day, the foundation gives way. When sin becomes known, others are hurt. Sin desires to take

Discernment 1

more than you ever thought you would give. Do you have any unrepentant sin patterns in your life? Are you walking with the Lord and increasing in holiness? Be sure you have a foundation of godly living and victory over sinful habits before you take steps toward dating.

SATISFACTION IN CHRIST

Contentment is living as though a change in circumstances is not needed for fulfillment because the Lord is enough. While writing Philippians, Paul was in hard circumstances. He was imprisoned (Phil. 1:7–12) and his life endangered (2:21). He reflects on the surpassing worth of Christ compared to any other aspect of life because Jesus is Lord (2:1–11; 3:8). The result is that Paul is content, no matter the external circumstances. When life is good and abundant, he can be content in Christ compared to material and relational abundance. When life is difficult and oppressed, he can be content in Christ (4:10–13). Contentment in Christ (or satisfaction in Christ) is especially evident when our circumstances do not align with our desires. One area in which people often feel discontentment is with money and possessions. They desire more money and possessions than they currently possess. When it comes to money and possessions, the pathway to contentment is the same. Hebrews 13:5–6 says: "Keep your life free from love of money, and be content with what you have, for he has said, "I will never leave you nor forsake you." We can be content because we already have the riches of God's presence in our lives.

How does God-fueled contentment translate to discerning your dating readiness? Is there part of your heart that perceives a boyfriend or girlfriend as the means to fulfillment? Just like freedoms of life in Philippians or money in Hebrews can be elevated above contentment in Christ, so can the longing for a dating and marriage relationship. It is perfectly ok to desire dating and, ultimately, marriage. In that desire, be conscious of how culture presents those relationships as a means to fulfillment. Movies, music, and the prevailing sexual ethic all proclaim a message that relationships and sex are necessary for completion as a human being. Such a claim is directly counter to the biblical framework for how to have healthy relationships. Looking at the culture around us also provides an inherent warning. Real-life examples abound, demonstrating that finding contentment in relationships does not ultimately satisfy. This is because Jesus Christ is the only person who can provide the needed fulfillment.

The lesson for relationships is the same as we find in Philippians and Hebrews. The God of the universe is the only one capable of satisfying your soul. Treasure knowing Christ and walking with Him as the supplier of contentment. The meaning of marriage is that human union provides a picture of God's union with humanity in salvation. The meaning of singleness is that Christ is sufficient to complete any person. While marriage is a good thing in God's design, no relationship is essential to contentment. This is why Jesus and Paul affirm singleness as a viable pathway for followers of Jesus (Matt. 19:10-12; 1 Cor. 7). Establish your contentment in Christ before you set out on a dating journey.

DISCIPLESHIP

The purpose of the Christian life is to be a faithful disciple and make faithful disciples. The best way to ensure you have the right priorities in dating and potential marriage is to live those priorities before you get started in a relationship. When it comes to being a disciple, an often-overlooked facet of following Christ is if you have someone intentionally investing in you. Do you have an older man or woman in your church who regularly invests in your life? This person might be called a mentor, disciple-maker, Bible study leader, or another title. The intent is to have someone with a perspective on your life to encourage you when you are discouraged, to teach you the Word of God, to warn or correct you in error, and to motivate you to persevere in faithfulness. For dating, the value is having someone who can help you assess if you are ready to date. We do not have a complete and unbiased view

Discernment 1

of ourselves regarding the criteria above. Wisdom welcomes the feedback and guidance of a wise and older brother or sister in your church who can speak truth in love to you (Prov. 19:20-21).

Not only should you be discipled by others, but you should also serve others by investing in their spiritual growth. A formal role and title are not required. Making disciples is using what the Lord has given you to influence others toward Christlikeness. Serving your church in this way before dating is important because it sets a trajectory of keeping the Great Commission at the center of life. Relationships that start without a balance of God's priorities tend to become all-consuming, and even with good intentions, squeeze out the things God says matter most. Prioritizing serving the Lord as the disciple-maker He calls you to be before dating will set a trajectory of the right ministry priorities as you date and potentially enter marriage. Are you being discipled by and discipling others in your local church? Set a trajectory of Great Commission ministry that transcends future dating relationships.

How do circumstances influence readiness?

There are circumstantial considerations about dating as well. Remember, the purpose of dating is to gain discernment regarding the potential of marriage ultimately. That is not to say first dates should jump to conclusions and be filled with awkward talk about marriage! At the same time, first dates result in deciding if there will be a second date, and so on it goes toward the ultimate destination (if all goes well). That means it's not wise to start if you are not in a place to follow through. One factor to consider is your life timeframe. Are you able to pursue marriage in a reasonable timeframe as it relates to factors like academic progress, finances, or parent expectations if a relationship goes well? If not, it may be wise to exercise patience and continue pursuing the right things as you wait for the right time. A word of balance is also in order when it comes to judging circumstances. Circumstances are never perfect. We are not saying that just because everything is not perfectly aligned with your preconceived expectations (or perhaps your parents' expectations), dating would be wrong. Circumstances need to be assessed with balance and wise counsel.

Conclusion

The single you will become the married you. Ensure that you are in a position to be able to contribute to a God-honoring relationship meaningfully. You might be wondering who can ever be ready to date. The trends are those who should not date jump right in without assessment, and those who are ready to date never take the leap because they do not think they are ready. The balance is approaching your circumstances with sobriety and seriousness because relationships are significant. At the same time, do not overcomplicate it. No one is ever perfectly ready. No person possesses perfect character. Be willing to uncompromisingly set the right trajectory for yourself before you begin dating. Also, be willing to jump into the adventure and embrace the risk of a relationship where you do not know the outcome. Be wise and intentional without being frozen in fear or overanalyzing.

Reflection Questions

1. Which of the assessment points above are your strengths and in which you should continue in faithfulness?
2. Which of the assessments above are weaknesses that might indicate you are not ready to date?
3. What plan can you make to grow in your points of weakness?
4. Who in your church can you invite into your life as a disciple-maker influence and voice of wisdom regarding dating?

20

Discernment 2

What should I look for in a spouse?

Nearly everyone has heard from a friend or family member, "Why don't you date him/her?" Sometimes, the answer is so self-evident that you say, "Not a chance." Then, what follows is often an explanation of why you ought to date that person. Sometimes, the argumentation is persuasive, but often, your mind was made up from the beginning. What are some good criteria or categories to think about when you are thinking about dating?

We have argued that dating is about discernment of God's call to marriage and to whom. Let's assume that you have read the previous chapters and you understand marriage and dating rightly, you have the proper goals in dating, and you are ready to date. We still need to think through the kinds of things to look for in someone we might date. What follows are some categories to think about drawn from biblical texts and wisdom from years in ministry to young adults.

What qualities should I look for in a spouse?

MATURING CHRISTIAN FAITH

The goal of dating is a God-honoring marriage. One historic statement of the faith has said that "the chief end of man is to glorify God and enjoy him forever."[1] That is an appropriate

---

1.   This is the first question of *The Westminster Shorter Catechism.*

summary of the overriding biblical command: "whatever you do, do all to the glory of God" (1 Cor. 10:31). If the heartbeat of the Christian is to glorify God, the most important quality in someone whom a Christian would marry is that that person seeks to glorify God with his or her whole heart. When Christians value some other characteristic or group of characteristics over a person's faith, they demonstrate what is really most important to them. As a Christian, Christ is the greatest priority in your life, so seek someone who shares your greatest priority.[2] Too often, people view physical beauty as the only or most important quality in a potential spouse. But more important than physical beauty is godliness: "Charm is deceitful, and beauty is vain, but a woman who fears the LORD is to be praised" (Prov. 31:30).

One way that the Bible talks about a person's closest relationships is to talk about a yoke. A yoke was a way to join together a pair of oxen to pull in the same direction. The Bible uses this imagery to command Christians, "Do not be unequally yoked with unbelievers" (2 Cor. 6:14). The idea is that the heart and life direction of a Christian and non-Christian are fundamentally different, so they will necessarily pull in different directions. In a close relationship, the Christian and non-Christian lack the most fundamental compatibility of being "in Christ." Hence, the Bible instructs the unmarried to marry "only in the Lord" (1 Cor. 7:39).

Let us give one more qualification. Look for demonstrated faith that is maturing. You do not want to marry someone who merely claims to be a Christian. You want to marry a genuine

---

2. Our assumption here is that we are addressing people who have the ability to choose whom they date and ultimately marry. We recognize that across cultures and times that freedom does not always exist. We also want to state that we are addressing people who are not yet married. It is not uncommon for two non-believers to marry and then one of them to convert to Christianity. In that instance, Paul gives clear instructions: "To the rest I say (I, not the Lord) that if any brother has a wife who is an unbeliever, and she consents to live with him, he should not divorce her. If any woman has a husband who is an unbeliever, and he consents to live with her, she should not divorce him" (1 Cor. 7:12–13). Paul will instruct the unmarried only to marry believers (1 Cor. 7:39), but he affirms the legitimacy of a marriage between a Christian and non-Christian. And he instructs Christians in these "mixed-marriages" to remain faithful to that marriage.

Christian who has evidence of faith in his or her actions. There is a sense in which faith is an inward, unobservable reality, but that faith always produces some external fruit. Jesus talks about knowing the health of the tree by the fruit that it produces: "So, every healthy tree bears good fruit, but the diseased tree bears bad fruit. A healthy tree cannot bear bad fruit, nor can a diseased tree bear good fruit" (Matt. 7:17–18). To stick with the "fruit" metaphor, look for these observable qualities in a potential spouse: "But the fruit of the Spirit is love, joy, peace, patience, kindness, goodness, faithfulness, gentleness, self-control…" (Gal. 5:22–23). We would also counsel you to look for someone who is maturing in these qualities. A good, lifelong marriage will require a humble disposition to ongoing growth. Look for someone with the humility and desire to keep growing in godliness.

CHURCH ENGAGEMENT

When you are looking for someone with whom to make a lifelong commitment, look for current evidence of commitment. Specifically, you want to see evidence of someone being committed to a spiritual endeavor that is imperfect – just like a marriage will be an imperfect spiritual endeavor. One of the best places to observe this quality is in how someone relates to a local church.[3] In the local church, we are bound together in covenant with imperfect people with a purpose beyond any individual. Does the person in whom you are interested demonstrate that he/she is willing to bear with

---

3. Matt Chandler (*The Mingling of Souls: God's Design for Love, Marriage, Sex, and Redemption* [Colorado Springs: David C. Cook, 2015], 40–41) gives similar counsel: "As you consider the person you are physically attracted to, look for evidence of commitment in his or her life. Has he joined and become committed to a local church? Does she have a deepening relationship with a group of friends? How is his relationship with his family? I think church membership is a huge consideration, precisely because there is no such thing as a perfect church, and in our day and age in the West, we have so many options to choose from. Churches are full of sinners, so there will always be some messiness in a church. Churches are like families in that way. So when a person stays in a church for a long period of time, there is evidence that she has been able to see that everything's not perfect, but she nevertheless said, 'I'm going to stay. I'm going to try to make this work. My commitment is more important than my desire to run away.'"

another and remain committed even in challenging situations? In the church, you are also able to observe if someone has a disposition toward service. Particularly, as you observe the person serving those in different age groups, you get a window into how that person would serve his/her children and aging parents.

We also counsel you to look at the person's compatibility with your own church commitments. By way of an autobiographical example, my (Trent) extended family did not do this well. My grandmother belonged to one denomination, and my grandfather belonged to another denomination. On Sunday mornings, my grandfather went to church by himself while my grandmother took the kids to her church. They lacked compatibility with their church commitments, which hindered their ability to raise their children with their joint examples of engaging the local church. You might meet someone who is undoubtedly a maturing Christian, but there exists a fundamental and unchanging incompatibility between your church convictions. That incompatibility will set you up for unnecessary tension and challenges. A caution: do not press incidental preferences to this level. For example, the preference between hymns versus contemporary worship music is probably an area in which you can compromise. But convictions on things like pedo vs. credo baptism, male-only vs. female pastors, etc., might be convictions that would entail you to committing to different churches. Your goal is to have a marriage between two maturing Christians in which you commit together to a church in which you raise your children together.

PHYSICAL ATTRACTION

Let's envision the situation in which a single Christian finds another single Christian who is clearly a maturing Christian with strong church involvement. But in this situation, there is no strong physical attraction. Is it OK, or wise, to pursue a dating relationship with someone to whom you are not attracted? There are several clarifications that are needed. Is

Discernment 2

physical attraction completely absent, or is it just not quite as strong as the person imagined it ought to be? Sometimes, people have an understanding of attraction imported from Hollywood, which demands adjectives like "breathtaking" or "stunning" to be present in order for attraction to be viewed as *real*. That definition of physical attraction is neither *realistic* nor sustainable. No marriage that has stood the test of decades has been an uninterrupted romance of physical attraction.

With those caveats, physical attraction is an aspect of marriage.[4] God created humans with inclinations toward physical attraction. One of the things that distinguishes marriage from all other relationships is that marriage is a sexual union, and physical attraction is an aspect of sexual union. While some of the idioms for physical beauty might be culturally different, Song of Songs 4–7 celebrate the physical attraction that an engaged couple and then a married couple have with one another. These chapters begin: "Behold, you are beautiful, my love, behold, you are beautiful! Your eyes are doves behind your veil. Your hair is like a flock of goats leaping down the slopes of Gilead" (Song 4:1). The Bible can celebrate physical attraction among this couple because God created the husband and the wife to be attracted to one another.

While we recommend physical attraction as a quality of a dating relationship, we also want to say that attraction and beauty are deeper than merely external qualities. The Bible describes beauty as not merely physical but rather the beauty of a heart set on God. Here are Peter's instructions to wives: "Do not let your adorning be external—the braiding of hair and the putting on of gold jewelry, or the clothing you wear— but let your adorning be the hidden person of the heart with the imperishable beauty of a gentle and quiet spirit, which in God's sight is very precious" (1 Pet. 3:3–4; see also 1 Tim. 2:9–10). The person who loves the things that God loves

---

4. We do not mean that a marriage cannot be sustained in the absence of physical attraction. Rather, we are giving counsel to those thinking about entering into marriage.

will find godly character beautiful and might find that his or her physical attraction grows as well. To state this clearly, attraction is more than a physical formula or a composite of certain physical features, and attraction can grow over time. The wife of decades can be more attracted to her balding and slightly out-of-shape husband than she was when he was in the prime of physical fitness with a flowing head of hair. And the same goes for a husband's attraction to his wife.

RECIPROCATED DESIRE

Marriage is a mutual commitment, so dating should have mutual desire. And many marriage laws in the United States articulate the need for consent. That is, both parties must be capable of making the commitment and are doing so by their own desires, free from coercion. Regrettably, some people forget this when they are pursuing a dating relationship. That is not to say that someone cannot change his or her mind, so that an initial "no" might someday become a "let's see." For example, a relationship that begins as a friendship might grow into something else. But this cannot be forced, and when a "no" or "not now" is given, the suitor needs to step back and provide space. You might choose to be patient to see if something develops, but do not be overbearing, obsessive, or unreasonably confident that a change of desires will occur.

SHARED INTENTIONS AND HOPES

This category is somewhat subjective, as a person's intentions and hopes can change. However, it is important to consider if one or both of the partners have certain non-negotiable intentions that are fundamentally incompatible with the other person. Let's envision, for example, a young man who has been called as a pastor in a local church and envisions himself serving that church for his lifetime. He develops a relationship with a godly young lady who senses a call to foreign missions. There is so much that is compatible in their trajectories, and they might find that God shapes their desires to align. But if they are both completely inflexible and unwavering in their plans, then it might not be the wisest to move forward with the relationship as long as these inflexible incompatibilities exist. Other areas to consider include the size of the family, living location, etc.

What qualities should I look for in a husband or wife, specifically?

The counsel we have provided so far has been applicable to both men and women. Look for a maturing Christian, involved in the local church, to whom you are attracted, and with whom you share similar life goals. But what counsel is unique to seeking a husband as distinct from seeking a wife? The particular qualities that one seeks in a potential husband or wife depend significantly on one's view of distinctions between men and women. Transparently, we want to state that we take a complementarian position in which we affirm that (1) men and women are equally created in the image of God and recreated in Christ by grace through faith, and (2) men and women are created with inherent distinctions that correspond to distinctions in roles, particularly expressed within the home and church. So take this as the kind of counsel we would give our students and children whom we have instructed with this view of Christian manhood and womanhood.

QUALITIES OF A HUSBAND

Some of the distinct calls to husbands are to lead, provide, and protect.[5] Here are some ways to look for these qualities in a potential husband. As a leader, how does this young man move things toward good? Does he exert a positive influence on those around him? Does his presence in a group of people push the group toward godliness and progress? As a provider, does he demonstrate a disposition to take responsibility for others' flourishing? Have you observed him being responsible

---

5.   A fuller explanation can be found here: Trent A. Rogers, "An Approach to Teaching my Son about Biblical Manhood" (*Journal of Human Behavior in the Social Environment* [2019], 1–14.

and handling money wisely? Does he demonstrate a work ethic and a drive to pursue things with vigor? Does he foster environments in which others flourish spiritually? As a protector, does he demonstrate inclinations to keep others from harm, or does he harm others (e.g., gossip or slander)? Are people merely a means for him to achieve his desires, or does he defend people as possessing inherent dignity? Here are some summary questions. If you had sons, would you be proud if they had the character and dispositions of this man? If the men in your local church had the character and dispositions of this man, would the church be a thriving spiritual community?

QUALITIES OF A WIFE

Some of the unique qualities of a wife are to respect others, nurture others, and receive leadership. Does she demonstrate a disposition to respect leadership (Eph. 5:33; 1 Pet. 3:2), or does she have a critical spirit? You might look at how she interacts with her parents. Does she nurture others with tender-hearted care? Part of what you are discerning is what she might be like as a mother. Have you observed her expressing care for others without recognition or being asked? Do others recognize her as a helper? Does she demonstrate a disposition to receive leadership? Does she willingly place herself under leadership in the local church or has she neglected that commitment? Have you seen her demonstrate that she can follow humbly and actively? As a summary question, would you want your daughters to be like her and interact with leadership like she does?

Conclusion

Discernment is not easy, especially when it involves the potential of a lifelong commitment. Nevertheless, God's Word gives us counsel on qualities to seek in a spouse. One more piece of counsel: do not treat this counsel as a checklist to grade someone. While some things are non-negotiable (e.g., clearly a committed Christian), other qualities might be those

Discernment 2

that are increasing in measure (e.g., developing a disposition of provision). The qualities we have outlined above should be taken alongside the counsel of your local church. God gives us the local body of believers to help us see clearly and discern prayerfully.

Reflection Questions

1. What is one area that you might have been overlooking in discerning a future spouse?
2. As you have practiced dating in the past, what have you prioritized? Are there changes in priorities that you need to make moving forward?
3. What are some areas in which you need to grow in order to become the kind of person that another maturing Christian would want to date?
4. Who is an older person in your church you could dialogue with about your potential dating partners to ensure careful consideration?

Conclusion

We have covered territory spanning diverse areas of life. The book's first section emphasized the importance of seeking wisdom from God's Word to develop a thriving spiritual life. The theme was to rightly respond to the work of Christ in faith not only at conversion, but throughout a life characterized by habits of Bible intake, prayer, and church community. Such habits will not disappoint. Our second section explored the ultimate purpose in life and focused on how to discern your particular ways of serving the Lord in life and career. Ordering our lives by God's purposes frees us to glorify Him in all our vocational pursuits. Our third section pierced through key cultural confusions of our times. Thinking with biblical discernment about significant issues provides a grounding for personal faith and the ability to represent Christ well to the world. Our fourth section focused on developing relationships in alignment with God's design. College is a season that can be filled with new and wonderful relationships, including dating on the way to potential marriage. College can also be fraught with difficulty in relationships when we depart from God's design. What unifies all these topics is an undergirding reality that God's Word provides wisdom for everything in life.

The twenty questions we explored all lead to one overarching question: what will you do with the truth of God's Word you have received? Turning to the correct place for answers is only part of the process. Wisdom received but not implemented will not result in deep roots. The Word of God must be received in soil of a heart that acknowledges God's truth and seeks to implement it faithfully. When the Word of God is taken into us through our eyes and ears, it is planted within us, and when it is met with faith-filled obedience on our part, the result is God-given growth (James 1:21; 1 Pet. 1:23). In a practical sense, daily life is determined by decisions. Take in God's Word and decide to obey it in dependence on Him, even when it is not easy. Every day in college, you will make decisions. There is always something shaping our decisions. Sometimes, college students unwittingly make decisions according to culture, tradition, bare human logic, or feelings. In contrast, making decisions based on principles in the Word of God is how you send down roots, enabling you to grow and stand during difficult times. In the first year of college, you might make more decisions on your own than you have in your entire life up to college. Reaching mighty oak status is the accumulation of many small decisions. Day in and day out, choose the ways of the Lord over all that competes for your allegiance. Mighty oak trees do not grow overnight. Commit to steadily walking in the truth.

We recognize the twenty questions are only a start on the college journey. College will bring new experiences and new territory to navigate. You likely already have questions about life we did not cover. Along the way, new questions will emerge that have not yet even crossed your mind. Where will you turn for answers? We hope these chapters have demonstrated that God's Word is sufficient for any questions that will ever come your way. Knowing Christ through the Bible provides all we need to live life in a way that glorifies God and results in our joy. In new and uncertain moments, turn to God's Word. Decide to plant your life in the truth and be dedicated to it over the long haul. When you do and look back over life, the results will not disappoint you.

> He is like a tree planted by streams of water that yields its fruit in its season, and its leaf does not wither. In all that he does, he prospers (Ps. 1:3).

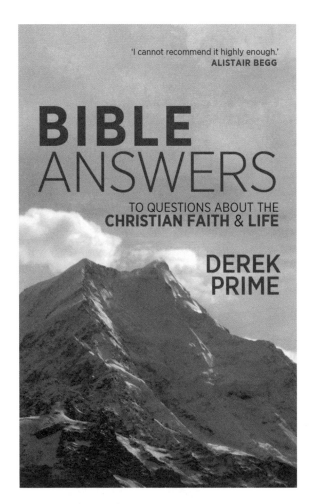

Bible Answers
by Derek Prime

Many people want to know what the Bible has to say about God and other pressing issues. To meet that need Derek Prime has provided a helpful guide that anyone can use. If you have ever wondered what the Bible really says about something, then this handy guide is where to look.

ISBN: 978-1-85792-934-8

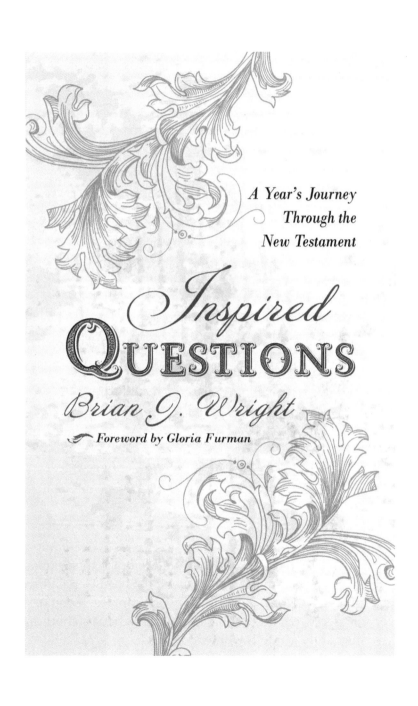

A Year's Journey Through the New Testament

Inspired Questions

Brian J. Wright

Foreword by Gloria Furman

Inspired Questions
by Brian J. Wright

Inspiring quotes and inspirational stories will always be popular, but they rarely change lives. After reading the quote, hearing the story, and experiencing some feelings, we often go about our business as usual. What we need is a spiritual resource that helps us focus on heart issues, life change, and the rhythm of the Christian life.

This year–long devotional takes 365 questions asked in the New Testament, and shows you how to change your focus, reorder your affections, and reprioritize your loves. It will inspire you to action, not just sweet reflections. It will compel you to love God and others more fervently and selflessly, while weaning your heart off the lies and lures of this world.

ISBN: 978-1-5271-0423-5

DAVID J. RANDALL

CHRISTIANITY

IS IT TRUE?

ANSWERING QUESTIONS
THROUGH REAL LIVES

Christianity: Is It True?

by David J. Randall

Here are twelve real–life heroes whose stories demonstrate the truth and relevance of the Christian faith. Their stories give answers to three questions many ask about Christianity:

- Is it true?

- Does it work?

- Is it worth it?

The lives of Columba of Iona, John Knox, John Bunyan, William Wilberforce, David Livingstone, Fanny Crosby, Mary Slessor, Corrie ten Boom, CS Lewis, Eric Liddell, Jim Elliot and Joni Eareckson Tada can inspire us because they did great things through faith.

ISBN: 978-1-5271-0236-1

edited by Glenn Myers

Susan Sutton
Evan Davies
Jean Goodenough
Glenn Myers
Jenny Davies
Byung Kook Yoo
Helen Roseveare
Patrick Johnstone
Daphne Spraggett

life
lessons
life-changing stories for christian growth

Life Lessons
edited by Glenn Myers

Nine people, all of them Christian workers with the mission agency WEC International, describe lessons that shaped and deepened their lives forever: Susan Sutton; Evan Davies; Jean Goodenough; Glenn Myers; Jenny Davies; Byung Kook Yoo; Helen Roseveare; Partick Johnstone; Daphne Spraggett.

Complete with study questions, and aimed for anyone wanting to grow in their Christian life, these stories are ideal either to read on your own or to discuss in a small group.

ISBN: 978-1-84550-555-4

Christian Focus Publications

Our mission statement
Staying Faithful

In dependence upon God we seek to impact the world through literature faithful to His infallible Word, the Bible. Our aim is to ensure that the Lord Jesus Christ is presented as the only hope to obtain forgiveness of sin, live a useful life and look forward to heaven with Him.

Our Books are published in four imprints:

◁◁✕ CHRISTIAN FOCUS

Popular works including biographies, commentaries, basic doctrine and Christian living.

◁◁✕ MENTOR

Books written at a level suitable for Bible College and seminary students, pastors, and other serious readers. The imprint includes commentaries, doctrinal studies, examination of current issues and church history.

◁◁✕ CHRISTIAN HERITAGE

Books representing some of the best material from the rich heritage of the church.

◁◁✕ CF4KIDS

Children's books for quality Bible teaching and for all age groups: Sunday school curriculum, puzzle and activity books; personal and family devotional titles, biographies and inspirational stories – because you are never too young to know Jesus!

Christian Focus Publications Ltd,
Geanies House, Fearn, Ross-shire,
IV20 1TW, Scotland, United Kingdom.
www.christianfocus.com